FOLLOWING THE
MARTIAL PATH

FOLLOWING THE MARTIAL PATH:

Lessons and Stories from a Lifetime of Training in Budo and Zen

WALTHER G. VON KRENNER

WITH KEN JEREMIAH

Foreword by

JOHN STEVENS

TAMBULI MEDIA

www.TambuliMedia.com
Spring House, PA USA

First Published on December 06, 2016 by Tambuli Media

ISBN-10: 0692818154
ISBN-13: 978-0692818152
Library of Congress Control Number: 2016961537

Edited by: Cindy Baldhoff
Cover and Interior by: Summer Bonne

TABLE OF CONTENTS

PUBLISHER'S FOREWORD

I believe that one of the greatest endeavors one can pursue is the journey of self-knowledge. And for me, and millions of others, the martial path is the journey of choice. The irony is that many martial artists who stay on their martial path for decades, even lifetimes, do not gain true self-knowledge; instead, they merely feed the ego. I have personally traveled the world many times in search of masters of martial, healing and spiritual practices, in the hope of becoming their apprentice and deepening my own self-understanding. But what I often encountered were masters and life-long students caught in the martial trap. That is, being so engrossed in the techniques of martial arts that all else is lost, ignored or underdeveloped. And so, it seems as if their path was not vertical but horizontal.

I find this not to be the case with Mr. Walther von Krenner, a man who began his martial journey a half-century ago in Germany, then traveled to the United States and then sold his house and moved to Japan to deepen his study and lengthen his journey. Von Krenner and I share many similarities on our paths of self-discovery, although he is much senior to me in the arts, having begun his journey before my birth. And while my journey led me to study indigenous practices of several countries, von Krenner's pursuits are wholly (and fully) within the arts of Japan.

Having lived in Japan, and having met some of the people von Krenner writes about in this book, it was a pleasure to read his moving accounts of living in Japan and, as an outsider, studying in martial and cultural arts. His accounts of what a class was like with Aikido founder Ueshiba and learning Ki development under Tohei sensei are remarkable. Not many were able to do this. I, for one, was refused an audience with Koichi Tohei when I wished to interview him at length about Ki development in Budo for a paper I was writing while at University.

Walther von Krenner has spent a lifetime in pursuit of self-knowledge through the practice and study of Budo, Zen, flower arranging, calligraphy, and more. A martial artist must be an artist in the broadest sense, he says, even including tea ceremony and sword appreciation and spiritual practices. I agree, especially when one wants to master the esoteric arts of an Asian country. One must immerse himself or herself in those studies, the country and its people and culture, and not merely show up twice a week at a local strip-mall dojo.

Von Krenner is unique today in that his time and place was such that he was able to be among the first Westerners to study under many of the 20th Century's greatest Japanese masters, including: Mori Terao (Kendo), Hideteka Nishiyama (Shotokan), Koichi Tohei (Ki), and Morihei Ueshiba, the founder and O-sensei of Aikido.

Some of my favorite books are those wherein we experience, as if directly, the teachings of masters we may never meet through the eyes of men who met and trained with them. Robert Smith's *Chinese Boxing: Masters and Methods*, Nigel Sutton's *Searching for the Way*, and Garry Parker's *Chanpuru: Lessons and Reflections from the Dojo*, are a few such books. And now we have Walther von Krenner's *Following the Martial Path*, wherein the reader is treated to his personal tales, vignettes, insights and reflections on all things relating to Budo and the Japanese classical traditions. I am honored to publish this book.

Circling back to my opening statement that many who follow the martial path do not gain depth of self-knowledge begs the question of why this may be the case. Well, von Krenner's opening paragraphs of this book's Introduction gives rhyme and reason in its analogy of colors and their many shades. So please read on, immerse yourself in this wonderful book. Experience the vast, almost endless "shades of gray" that present on the path of martial arts and personal excellence. Let Walther von Krenner show you a way forward by allowing you a rare keyhole into what it is like to learn at the hands of so many of the world's most famous Japanese masters; many of whom are no longer with us.

Dr. Mark Wiley
Publisher, Tambuli Media

FOREWORD BY JOHN STEVENS

$\mathcal{F}$ollowing the Martial Path: Lessons and Stories from a Lifetime of Training in Budo and Zen is Walther von Krenner's rollercoaster account of his fifty years of training in Budo. He had the good fortune to train and learn from many of the outstanding martial art masters of the 20th century. For example, he studied kendo with Mori Terao, grappled with "Judo Gene LaBelle," trained in Shotokan karate with Nishiyama Hidetaka, and explored the mysteries of ki with Tohei Koichi. However, Walther's primary teacher and guiding light was Ueshiba Morihei, the founder of Aikido. He is one of the last remaining non-Japanese students who actually trained with Morihei in Japan.

Walther's quest for the true meaning of Budo is presented in many tales throughout the book. Some are classical, others personal. Such tales are both entertaining and enlightening. Walther makes the key point that a martial artist should be an artist in the broadest sense: a student of literature and poetry, and (in his case) a practitioner of such disciplines as calligraphy, painting, shakuhachi playing, sword connoisseurship, and tea ceremony. Many of the illustrations in this book are creations by Walther. Walther's spiritual grounding is in Zen meditation, esoteric cosmology, and Aikido philosophy. All three aspects are discussed in detail.

Walther is opinionated, gruff, and not one to tolerate foolishness or pusillanimity. From his unique perspective, he tells and shows us "how it is," through the use of text and illustrations. Following the Martial Path is altogether a stimulating and challenging book.

INTRODUCTION

*O*riginally, the Japanese language did not have a term for green. The word *ao* referred to both blue and green. The colors were so close that they were just considered different shades. This might seem strange to speakers of other languages, but lexicon varies between cultures. In the English language, for example, there is only one word for gray, even though there are many shades of gray. To an unobservant person, they might all look the same, but to someone who looks carefully, there are countless variations, all of which are distinct colors. When practitioners begin studying a martial art, they might not even see gray. They might see everything in black and white. There are no great mysteries. Everything is as it appears.

Techniques are nothing more than devices used to control or injure another. Most students do not progress beyond this point. They perform throws and pins, and thinking there is nothing more to learn, they stop studying. Those who continue training might eventually master the techniques, and with that mastery comes a new perception: a new way to see things. What were once regarded as two separate colors, black and white, blend together. Practitioners begin to see gray. The techniques are more than just physical motions. They contain profound principles. Once this realization occurs, they are pulled into the wormhole, and what started out as simple becomes incredibly complex. What began as an awareness that there is more than just black and white, that there is gray, eventually leads to the conclusion that there are countless variations of gray. The martial arts have multiple shades: different teachings, which can only be perceived through years of hard training. This is *shugyo*. It is interesting that the more one trains, the more he or she realizes how much there is to learn. There is no end in sight. What starts out as physical techniques used to protect oneself and defeat others, becomes something more: devices to forge and polish the spirit.

A connection exists between Zen and the martial arts. If practitioners view things in the correct manner, many different paths lead to the same destination. This is why some Japanese masters not only practice martial arts, but also practice skills like *ikebana* (flower-arranging), *shodo* (calligraphy), *bijutsu* (art), or *sado* (the Way of Tea), learning from the stark simplicity yet whole-minded effort of the *cha no yu* (tea ceremony). All of these pursuits are Budo, and they reflect the Japanese expression *bun bu ryo do*: the way of the brush is the same as the way of the sword. All of these pursuits are manifestations of Zen.

Over the years, I have continued to train in Zen meditation, calligraphy, painting, the tea ceremony, and the martial art Aikido, and I continue to progress on the path. I began my martial training in Germany more than fifty years ago, learning Judo from Heinreich Steffin, Kondo Mitsuhiro (ninth dan) and Nagaoka Hidekaru (tenth dan). After winning in my class at the national championship in 1959, I traveled to France to train in Judo at the Salle Pleyel Dojo, where tenth-dan Anton Geesink taught. He was a three-time World Judo champion, an Olympic gold medalist, and he won twenty-one European Judo championships. Many great martial artists trained at this dojo.

In 1960, I left France and moved to the United States to train at Hal Sharp's dojo, where ninth-dan Gene LeBell trained. He has written many books and has been in more than one thousand movies and television shows. Training with LeBelle was difficult, and I learned a lot. At about the same time, I also began learning karate from Nishiyama Hidetaka. While training at Hal Sharp's dojo, I was also teaching at David Chow's dojo, who was the Hong Kong Judo champion. David Chow's dojo was located at the Encino Community Center, where I experienced Aikido for the first time.

One day, when I arrived at the dojo, many people were present and chairs were set up. The Judo class had been canceled because there was going to be a demonstration of a new martial art called Aikido. I sat down to watch, and people with kendo gear (i.e. hakama) were flying through the air, taking what I perceived as unrealistic falls. The instructor wore glasses, and his hair remained perfectly in place as he repeatedly threw his attackers to the ground.

I knew it had to be fake, and I was a little unhappy that my class was canceled; I really wanted to train. After the demonstration, the instructor, Ueshiba Kisshomaru, held a question-and-answer session. I told him that such techniques would probably not work on a Judo practitioner, and he invited me to attack. I did, and Ueshiba sprained my wrist using kotegaeshi. Thinking it had to be a fluke, I attacked with the other hand, and he busted that one too. After this incident, I wanted to learn as much about Aikido as I could.

1. Signed photograph of Ueshiba Kisshomaru Sensei, who first introduced me to Aikido

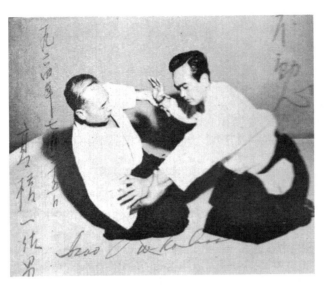

2. Signed photograph of Takahashi Isao Sensei

Ueshiba Sensei remained in the United States for about four weeks, during which time I trained with him. When the time came for him to return to Japan, he introduced me to Takahashi Isao, with whom I practiced for years. We not only trained in his dojo, but also practiced techniques in his backyard or garage, trying to perfect even the smallest details. We did a lot of ki training, and we frequently talked about the sword and its connection to Aikido. I was interested in the Japanese sword, and at the time, I was president of the Japanese Sword Society, a group whose members share a passion for historical scholarship and research. He often came to my house and we spent hours talking about swords, Aikido and even calligraphy. Then we trained in my private dojo. He even taught me how to play the Japanese flute, the *shakuhachi*.

Takahashi Sensei introduced me to Tohei Koichi, the man who did more than anyone else to disseminate Aikido to the world. Aikido would not have taken root in the United States without his efforts, and I believe he was the most important person in the development of Aikido as a martial art distinct from Daito-ryu Aikijujutsu. Tohei even developed the names of the techniques used today. The founder, O-Sensei, use terms like *ude osae*, *kote mawashi*, and *kote hineri* to describe techniques. Tohei Sensei simplified these so foreigners could more easily remember them. He replaced them with words more recognizable today, such as *ikkyo*, *nikkyo*, and *sankyo*: literally, "technique number one, two, and three." Tohei Sensei stressed the importance of ki, and he taught me how to use it in my training. Practitioners today might look at some old pictures of O-Sensei, in which many students pushed on his head or chest while he was either seated on the ground or standing, and wonder how it was done. Such performances might look like magicians' tricks to an out-side observer, but they are a demonstration of ki power. Tohei Sensei taught me how to do these techniques so I could teach others about ki and convince skeptics about this energy source's existence.

3. Signed photograph of Tohei Koichi

While training with both Tohei Sensei and Takahashi Sensei, I met many interesting people who today are considered experts in Japanese martial arts. These include Don Angier and Meik Skoss, who was a beginner student in our San Fernando Valley Dojo. However, I had not yet trained with the art's founder. In 1967, Takahashi Sensei came to my house and told me to go to Japan to train while O-Sensei was still alive. At the time, I was dealing Asian artwork, and I had a business called Art Treasures of Asia. I thought about it and decided that I did want to go, but the only way I could afford a trip like that was for my wife and me to sell our house. She was supportive, and that is what we did; we sold our home and moved to Japan so I could train with O-Sensei.

4. Signed photograph of O-Sensei

Japan at that time was much different than it is today. I arrived at Haneda airport and hailed a cab. I did not realize how far from Tokyo this airport was, but the exchange rate at the time was about 360 yen to a dollar, so even this long ride was inexpensive. I asked the driver to take me to the Aikido Hombu Dojo, and he had no idea what I was talking about. In the West, Aikido was well known, at least in our circles, and I had assumed that everyone in Japan was likewise acquainted with this new art. Apparently, this was not the case. I asked him to take me to Shinjuku. Today, this is a busy area of Tokyo; skyscrapers are everywhere, dwarfing the constant crowds of people who live there, but at the time, it was not as built up. The highest building was the Odakyu department store, and that was only three floors. You would be hard-pressed to find a building that only had three floors in Tokyo today. The taxi driver stopped in Shinjuku and asked a passerby if he knew where the Aikido dojo was located. His response was, "What is Aikido?" Suddenly, the name of the specific street where the dojo was located came to mind: wakamatsu-cho. The driver took me there. The road itself was only about seven feet wide, so the car could not enter. I got out, paid the driver, and walked toward the dojo.

The exterior of the new Hombu Dojo in Tokyo today looks like a department store or an office building, but when I went there to train, it was different. It was pretty. Two stone pillars seemingly held the surrounding wall at bay, and a garden path led to the dojo entrance. It was a Japanese-style garden, with moss, stones, plants and trees. On one of the pillars was a sign, which read "Aikido Hombu Dojo." The main entrance was a Japanese-style sliding door. By the time I arrived, it was already evening. Assuming that classes were about to start soon, I slid open the door and stepped inside into the *genkan*, or entryway, where I took my shoes off. The dojo itself had about fifty or sixty (tatami) mats. It was quiet because no one was there.

The sliding doors on the other side of the mats opened and Ueshiba Kisshomaru appeared. Noticing that someone was in the dojo, he walked quickly toward me, but as he approached, he recognized me. He shook my hand and explained that there were no classes in the evening, only in the morning. He pointed the way toward the dormitory across the street, a two-story building with twelve rooms. My good friend, Dr. Robert Frager, had a room on the first floor, and said I could move in with him. Bob was a former professor at Harvard University, and trained in Aikido, Judo, and Karate. (He and I later attended the same conference on East Asian Studies at the University of Hawaii.) Eventually, someone upstairs moved out and it was a better room, so Bob moved into it, leaving me alone on the first floor. My room was only six tatami mats in size, and the futon was so small that my feet stuck out. I had to have another one made just so my entire body would fit on the bedding. But upon arriving in Japan, I was at least happy to have a place to stay, and I looked forward to meeting the master in the morning.

5. Hombu Dojo, Shinjuku-ku, 102 Wakamatsu-cho (1967)

O-Sensei was not at the dojo every day. However, on this particular day, he was there, and after class, Bob led me to his office. The door was so low that I had to get onto my knees to enter. In my hand was a letter of introduction from Takahashi Sensei. Upon seeing it, O-Sensei began talking. His high-pitched voice had an ethereal, transcendental quality. He talked for about a half hour that day and although I did not understand everything he said, I never forgot it.

I trained in Japan for the last two years of O-Sensei's life, and I learned a lot. In this book, I hope to convey some of the lessons I learned to other practitioners. Some great photographs that I have compiled through the years appear in this text. Alongside such photographs are examples of calligraphy and paintings that I did. To me, such art forms are just as much a part of Budo training as Aikido and Judo are. They are Zen practices, illustrating the core principles found in this way of life. When I was in Japan, I thought it was important to record as many speeches and sayings of the founder as possible, so that this knowledge could be passed down to future generations. I kept a three-volume journal in which I recorded his lessons, my interpretation of the message conveyed and some artwork that I thought best reflected the ideas. Some of these are also included in this text. I hope students on the path find them beneficial.

Ueshiba Morihei O-Sensei admonished, "Never consider yourself an all-knowing, perfected master; you must continue to train daily with your friends and students and progress together." And he practiced what he preached. Until his death, he consistently trained. He never stopped and I continue to emulate him. Following his example, I train daily, trying to improve my Aikido and myself. I do not consider myself an all-knowing master, but having walked the road of traditional Budo for more than fifty years, and having studied under many of the world's great teachers, I feel entitled to make some observations. I offer them here, in this text, in the hope that they will assist others who follow the same path.

6. Dragon rising over Mt. Fuji, (after Tesshu).
I have painted another, which depicts a snail climbing Mt. Fuji. The dragon
gets there in one leap. The snail moves slowly and works hard, but it also
reaches the top.

CHAPTER 1:
FROM ANCIENT TO MODERN MARTIAL ARTS

*D*uring the *sengoku jidai*, or Warring States Period, which lasted from the middle of the fifteenth century to the beginning of the seventeenth century, constant conflicts plagued Japan. Warriors perfected their skills, as their abilities were a matter of life and death. When samurai went into battle, there was a good chance that they would not return. On the battlefield, being attacked from all directions with weapons like swords, spears, and halberds, survival was difficult. Even up against just one opponent, survival was doubtful. It has been said that a warrior only had a thirty-three percent chance of returning when fighting a single person. If he were better than his opponent, he would defeat him and go home. If the opponent were better, he would be killed. And if they were equally skilled, they would both die, for as soon as one warrior spotted an opening, a weakness in his opponent's defenses, he would exploit it, thus revealing a weakness in his own defenses. This resulted in *aiuchi*, or mutual death.

During these times, martial techniques were tested and perfected. Samurai who used ineffective techniques did not return from battle. They died, and their combative methods were snuffed out. Martial techniques from this period that are still around today were effective. Warriors who consistently survived great battles became teachers. Others recognized their skills and wished to learn from them. In this way, martial art schools began. Due to the real possibility of fighting for one's life, dojo at this time were much different from dojo today. Walking into many different classes, whether the martial art taught is Aikido, Kyudo, Kendo, or others, a visitor might get the idea that they are supportive, safe places. This is because there is no realistic possibility of death. The arts will not have to be used for survival. During the Warring States Period, death was a constant possibility. If a practitioner's skill was lacking, if he had the wrong angle with a sword, or if his *maai* (combative space) was faulty, he would be defeated. He would be killed.

Today, dojo instructors will typically not be challenged. When they demonstrate techniques, their students do not fight them. They go along with pins and throws, sometimes taking unrealistic falls or crying out in pain, when no real pain is applied. The martial arts have become demonstrative, something for the movies rather than actual techniques used to stay alive. In the fifteenth and sixteenth century, martial art instructors were challenged constantly. Skilled swordsmen traveled the country looking for challenges. They showed up at dojo and asked for a match. And if they defeated the head instructor, the dojo would become theirs. Sometimes, they would take over and become the head instructors. Other times, they would burn the building to the ground and move on to the next one. This was called *dojo yaburi*: tearing apart a dojo.

These were difficult times. The possibility of death was real, and warriors trained to avoid it. They often engaged in meditative disciplines, attempting to eliminate fear, as fear could have an adverse effect on fighting skills. To develop the right mindset for combat, warriors often turned to religious or spiritual practices. Many turned to Zen, a Buddhist sect that stresses self-reliance. Other samurai engaged in Shinto-based practices to attain a state of mind that would benefit them in combat. It was not enough to remove the fear of death. They also had to be able to kill. In modern dojo, martial arts are typically thought of as self-defense. Traditionally, defense was a part of the martial arts. But offense also had to be there. It was the samurai's job to kill, so while practicing, he not only had to perfect his blocks and parries, but also his killing moves. He had to perfect his feints, cuts and thrusts, so that once his opponent reacted to his motion, the response would lead to his death. These two interrelated mindsets are difficult to acquire: being unconcerned about your own death, and being comfortable while killing another. Two things were necessary to attain such a mindset: engaging in life and death battles, and practicing meditation. *Zazen*, seated meditation, is stressed in Zen Buddhism, and it was the religion of choice for many warriors. Strangely, they did not study it to become priests or to become more spiritual, but to become better fighters.

In 1600, the Tokugawa defeated the Toyotomi at the famous Battle of Sekigahara, which took place in Gifu Prefecture. Having brought the different provinces together under one rule, there was a period of relative peace and stability. The Tokugawa Shogunate issued the *sakoku* edict, which banned foreigners from the country. It outlawed Christianity, moved the capital to Edo, modern day Tokyo, and established the *sankin kotai* system. Formalized in 1635, it required each *daimyo* (feudal lord) to spend half of his time in the capital. When he was not there, his wife and heir had to remain as hostages. In this way, the Tokugawa maintained the daimyo's allegiance, and peace prevailed.

As there was no longer a need to kill and protect oneself on a battlefield, the arts changed during this period. Many became more formalized, and how they looked to observers became more important than martial efficacy. Practitioners of the old arts trained with the idea that they were facing samurai wearing armor, so they targeted the armor's weak points. During the Edo period, martial artists were not up against people wearing armor, so a much wider range of targets became available. In addition, empty-handed arts, like jujutsu, became more popular. Jujutsu was also known as *yawara, taijutsu, shubaku, hakuda, torite,* and *kogusoku*. Many of the techniques found in jujutsu styles from this period would not have worked on warriors wearing armor. New techniques became available, and methods of pinning and restraining individuals were perfected. Some arts made use of elaborate pins, in which not just one arm was controlled, but in which both arms and sometimes both legs were all controlled at once. Some of these pins are still seen in arts like Daito-ryu Aikijujutsu.

These Edoized arts continued to change. Some styles of jujutsu were used on battlefields, when samurai had lost their long sword. One still extant style is Takenouchi-ryu. It made use of jujutsu techniques up against an armor-wearing opponent. Once the warrior was in a disadvantageous position, a small knife was then used to kill. Most historical jujutsu techniques were always concluded with a killing thrust or cut. During the Edo Period, this finishing kill was eliminated from most arts. At the end of techniques, the person being pinned would tap, signifying that he had been effectively restrained. The mindset of practitioners naturally changed during this era, and the techniques they practiced were no longer killing techniques. They eventually became thought of as self-defense techniques alone.

As time progressed, this new martial outlook became commonplace, and the arts continued to change. In the Meiji Period (1868-1912), some arts became sports. Others were viewed as a means of self-improvement. What were once regarded as arts designed to kill and maim now became spiritual disciplines. The connection between Zen and Budo grew, and they were considered one and the same. A person could pursue various disciplines, but if his mindset was always aiming for self-realization, then all of the disciplines became paths to the same summit. Certainly, there are many ways to climb a mountain, but no matter what path one might take, he or she will eventually arrive at the only summit, the only goal.

Kano Jigoro (1860-1938), the founder of Judo, lived during the Meiji Period. He trained in an old style of jujutsu called Kito-ryu, and O-Sensei also trained in this art. He took some of the techniques from the old jujutsu styles and created a martial way. Linguistically, he removed the term jutsu (art), and replaced it with do (way). Ethically, he turned it into a system that stressed mutual cooperation and benefit. He perceived Judo as a perfect form of physical education, and the art is practiced in many Japanese high schools and universities. Kano was greatly admired; even the founder of Aikido looked up to him, and almost all martial arts have adopted the (kyu-dan) belt ranking system that he developed. Beyond physical education, Kano perceived the art as conducive to training the mind. *Randori* training or matches, are safe ways to practice originally dangerous techniques. Rules were developed to maintain safety, but if approached in the correct manner, the mindset of a warrior can be developed. Kano explained:

> *In randori, one can never be sure what technique the opponent will employ next, so he must be constantly on guard. Being alert becomes second nature. One acquires poise, the self-confidence that comes from knowing that he can cope with any eventuality. The powers of attention and observation, imagination, of reasoning and judgment are naturally heightened, and these are all useful attributes in daily life as well as in the dojo.[1]*

It is also a system of ethical training. Training in Judo can help people to control their anger. It can also help them to develop confidence and happiness. The true purpose of all modern forms of Budo is to better oneself, and to develop a mind-set that will enable practitioners to defend themselves no matter where they are or what they are doing. In other words, it helps them to be constantly aware: the presence of mind developed through Zen practices as well as martial arts. Kano explained:

[The essence of Judo] is contained in the saying: Walk a single path, becoming neither cocky with victory nor broken with defeat, without forgetting caution when all is quiet or becoming frightened when danger threatens. Implicit here is the admonition that if we let ourselves be carried away by success, defeat will inevitably follow victory. It also means that one should always be prepared for a contest — even the moment after scoring a victory. Whether a person's surroundings are calm or turbulent, he should always exploit whatever means are at hand to accomplish his purpose.[2]

Martial arts today are much different from the arts they once were, and it is important to keep in mind the transformation that occurred over hundreds of years. The same type of transformation occurs within each individual, provided that he or she trains in an appropriate manner. At first, practitioners learn techniques. It is not possible to access the spiritual and ethical dimensions of such arts without understanding the physical techniques that can be used to protect oneself or others. After learning these techniques, one must practice wholeheartedly for many years. Eventually, the techniques become natural. In time, if students are disciplined and continue to train sincerely, a spiritual element will naturally develop. This cannot be rushed nor bypassed. Kyudo teacher Onuma Hideharu wrote:

Technique is the stairway to the spiritual level. Students think of the study of technique as something they must endure, like some form of punishment dispensed by the teacher. They want to dispense with technique as soon as possible and move on to the more creative, spiritual aspects of study. But to learn technique you must carefully control the workings of your mind

and body. And that is what students misunderstand. Controlling
the mind and body does not stifle the spirit; it sets it free.[3]

Since the martial arts will likely not be used in contests of life and death today, each individual practitioner must make the decision to train as hard as possible. Those who do so improve quickly, and eventually master the arts that they study. Others who do not have such discipline can train for years yet not improve substantially. This is not some weakness inherent in the arts; it is a weakness in the individual practitioner, a weakness that he or she chooses not to eliminate. Real training is difficult. It takes constant effort. It requires self-reflection and a selfless approach to training. One must train with no thought whatsoever of pain and suffering. Students have to push themselves to rise above such distractors. This is shugyo.

Fudo Myoo
The Lotus bloom in the Fire, it is
because of the Fire the Lotus bloom.
J. Cummins.

7. The Sanskrit Seed-Syllable for Fudo-Myoo, one of the Guardian Kings of Buddhism. Mountain ascetics, who engaged in austere practices, shugyo, often invoked his presence.

CHAPTER 2:
SHUGYO

*F*or a time, my wife Hana and I lived near Lac de Constanza, known in English as Lake Constance. It has a surface area of 536 km2 (207 sq. mi) and joins Germany, Switzerland, and Austria. Our home was on Germany's side, and I was studying Judo with Heinreich Steffin, a talented teacher. He had a traditional dojo, and no girls were allowed inside. This was difficult for Hana, who would come to pick me up after class had ended. I trained hard, and I often did not want to stop. She would come at 10:00, and seeing that I was not yet finished, would return at 10:30, then 11:00, then 11:30, before finally giving up and going home. (She was extremely patient, and she has supported me every step of the way in my life of Budo training.) I have always wanted to learn and improve, so as long as my instructor was willing to keep teaching me, I stayed.

8. The dojo at Konstanz, Germany (c. 1958) I am in the back left.

9. Another picture from 1958. I was closest to the photographer.

10. My first teacher, Heinrich Steffin, performing the Ju no Kata. Egan Münk is uke (1958).

One extreme example of this persistence occurred while at Nagaoka Sensei's dojo. It was small, and we had to be careful when we trained because there was a post in the mat's center. While I was working on some throws with a partner, he approached me and said, "Stay after class and I will give you the secret of *tsukuri* for a Judo throw." This term meant "fitting in," and referred to entering into the opponent so that a throw could be applied successfully. Of course, I waited, and after everyone else had left, he walked off the mat and out of view. When he returned, he had a bicycle inner tube in his hand. He wrapped it around the post, held both sides of it with his hands, and then entered as though he were performing a hip throw. He demonstrated the correct movements several times, and then said, "Just keep doing this until you discover the secret." I kept at it, performing the same motion repeatedly. Eventually, I was so tired that I did not think I could continue. My knees were buckling and I could not stand up, but I pushed forward, through the pain. After hours, I had discovered the secret of entering. When I looked at the clock, it was 4:00 a.m. I had been at it for more than six hours!

**11. Nagaoka Sensei, my second Judo teacher, performing Yama Arashi.
Steffin Sensei is uke. (1958).**

12. Nagaoka Sensei of the Kodokan.
He was killed in a car accident while visiting us in Konstanz (1959). The small lapel pin is the Kodokan Sakura logo. We were so proud when we were allowed to wear this pin.

This is often the only way to learn, and it is a training method that has existed since the Warring States Period, when technical proficiency meant the difference between life and death. Kano Jigoro explained:

Once my master threw me with what would now be called a sumi-gaeshi (corner-throw). I didn't know how he did it, so I asked him. He said nothing and used the same technique on me again. So I begged him to explain to me how he had done it, whereupon he used the same technique on me once again. This time I asked him to explain in detail how to pull the arms, how to place the legs, and how far to lower the hips, without actually

John Stevens, in his book *The Way of Judo: A Portrait of Jigoro Kano and his Students*, explained that because Kano was a scholar and one of the most important educators in Japanese history, he initially began learning techniques from a scientific standpoint. However, this obsession with describing exact angles and body placement is not effective in the martial arts. The only way to gain practical knowledge is to experience the techniques firsthand.

Originally, the martial arts were not taught using detailed explanations. Instead, instructors demonstrated the techniques. They expected students to pay attention to what was occurring, and then to practice repeatedly until they could duplicate what their instructors had done. This type of instruction led to a type of seeing, a vision that some modern practitioners lack. Students who truly wished to become proficient had to learn how to see what was occurring, exactly what their teachers were doing. It was not enough to see just the external movement, they had to go home and meditate on the inherent principles that made the techniques work. This required self-discipline bordering on obsessiveness. Today, teachers explain the techniques, and as a result, some students become lackadaisical. They do not put forth great effort because they do not realize what they are missing. They train, and in a short time think that they have mastered the techniques of whatever art they are studying. A popular expression among Chinese martial artists is the following: "After three years of training, students start to think that they can conquer the entire world. In the next three years, they find it difficult to improve even a little bit." Students who have only been studying for several years start to believe that they are skilled, until they get a wake-up call. This is a natural progression, and no one skips steps. After years of training in Judo, I believed that I was great. My wake-up call came in France.

13. Have Nothing. Always keep your mind empty of preconceptions.

CHAPTER 3:
A LESSON IN HUMILITY

*A*s I trained, my Judo skills continued to develop. I bested many of the people I trained with, and I won several championships in southern Germany and Switzerland. In 1959, I competed in the German Judo Single Master Competition in Hamborn, and I won in my class.

14. Flyer for the Judo Championship in Hamborn, (1959).

The three winners, myself and two other friends, won a free trip to Paris. We were naturally excited. We were only about eighteen years old, and we had an opportunity to train at the famous Salle Pleyel Dojo, where almost all of the European champions trained at one time or another. My girlfriend Hana, who would later become my wife, packed a box of food for us, and we left Germany. After arriving in France, we went out to celebrate. We were on the Boulevard de Clichy, where the Moulin Rouge was located along with countless bars and clubs. We had a great time, although we might have had too much to drink.

We exited a bar and headed down the street toward our hotel. In front of us was a good-looking girl, wearing high heels, who was trying to walk along the cobblestone road. I came up behind her and put my arm around her, but before I could say anything, I found myself on the ground. She had thrown me, and if I had not known *ukemi*, how to fall, she might have injured or even killed me. That is how hard I hit the ground. Luckily, I had actually practiced ukemi on concrete back in Germany. Seeing me fall, she looked down at me and said, "You are a Judo guy, huh?"

I was still in shock, but I responded, "You're a Judo girl?"

"Yes," she said. "I am an instructor at Salle Pleyel."

We were supposed to train at this dojo. It was an awkward situation for me. At only eighteen years of age, having just won a championship, I was confident in my skills and I did not think a physically weaker girl could defeat me. I did not like this situation at all. Nevertheless, we made it back to our hotel, and I did not have any real injuries. My ego was a bit sore and I tried to fix it when I arrived at the dojo the next day.

A woman's class was being held on the third floor. The class was already in session and the girl who had thrown me the evening before was teaching. I approached her and said, "I would like to try this one more time."

She responded, "My technique worked when I needed it to work. I don't need anything beyond that."

Defeated, I headed downstairs to the second floor where the men's class was held. I was still confident in my abilities, and I knew that after working out with some of the people there, I would forget all about being thrown the evening before. Scanning the dojo, I saw a man in the corner who had just stepped onto the mat wearing a white belt. I thought to myself, "This guy would be a good person to warm-up with, since he's a beginner." We partnered up.

15. Practicing high-falls on concrete in Germany (1959). I am nage in this photo.

As soon as we made contact, I was on the ground. I was surprised because I considered myself a champion. How could this person throw me so easily? I got up, and he threw me again. And then again. I could not do anything to him. I was in shock and I had lost all confidence in my techniques. Later, I saw him in the locker room coming out of the shower. I said, "God, you are fantastic for a beginner."

He smiled a bit, and then responded, "You really don't know who I am, do you?"

I shook my head from side to side, and he said, "I am Jacques Courtin, three-time European champion." He had forgotten his black belt, so he borrowed a beginner's belt.

I realized that I was too focused on the color of his belt, and I did not pay attention to how he moved or how strong he was. I came to realize that rank, the color of one's belt, is completely insignificant compared to skill. And the color of a belt does not always accurately reflect a person's skill. Sometimes, beginners and other people who do not understand the old martial art ways (*kodo*) think that a title, hakama, or other outward symbols indicate that they are technically proficient and superior to others who do not have such symbols. This does not make sense. Just as I cannot become a cowboy by simply wearing a cowboy hat, or become a teacher because I state that I am a teacher, martial skills do not improve through rank. How can one even be a teacher, without first being a true student?

Takahashi Isao once said, "It is not the rank that makes the man, but the man who makes the rank." No matter how this lesson is worded, it always points to the same important conclusion: ranks are insignificant compared to skill. It is helpful to remember, too, that Ueshiba Morihei O-Sensei, along with the founders of many other well-known and respected martial traditions, did not have any rank. More than one million people worldwide studied Aikido while he was still alive, and yet he would still explain to the students in Japan who knew him personally that he was "still just a beginner." There is profound wisdom in this statement.

In Japan, Shimizu Sensei once told me, "After fifteen years you gain a slight understanding." In our time, we see so-called great experts arise after a short study in any given discipline. This is America, and it seems that people want traditional titles without traditional requirements. An example of this tendency is the much desired and illustrious black belt. Someone who wears this is nothing more than a senior student. He or she is not a teacher, just a student further along the path. A *shodan* is expected to act like an older sibling to the *mudansha* (unranked or junior students), and set a good example by adhering to dojo etiquette, tenets and traditions. At the same time, he or she must continue to work hard to improve martially, looking to *sempai* (people even further along the path) for guidance.

The ranking system in dojo today does serve a purpose. For people further along the path, ranks become insignificant, but for beginners who need milestones, the ranks can help them to gauge their progress. For some, rank tests become thought of as some of the most important milestones in their lives. Later, they see things differently, and realize that such examinations were ultimately important, but during the tests themselves, some people get extremely nervous. I also went through this phase; it is nothing unique. I remember a funny episode that occurred during a kendo test:

I used to love samurai shows, and when I was young one of my favorites was called *The Tiger of Kofu*. This series portrayed a samurai protagonist who was able to get in and out of many predicaments by using unorthodox methods. One episode showed the hero using a strange sword technique called the "Full Moon Cut." As a young, inexperienced martial artist and sword aficionado, I loved the technique. Later, when I was testing for shodan in sword, I was pitted against a much higher-ranking swordsman who wanted me to fail. When I faced him, all my training seemed to disappear, and the only thing left in my mind was the "fake" technique that I had seen in the samurai series. I did it. It was such an impractical move that my opponent did not expect it, and he dropped his guard. (He was probably wondering what the hell I was doing!) Once his guard dropped, I struck his helmet, screaming "*men*." My teacher, Mori Sensei, asked us to stop. He had a stern look on his face.

"You," he said, pointing. "Come here!"

I approached and bowed. "Where did you learn that?" he asked.

I was a bit nervous, but I had to tell him the truth. "From *The Tiger of Kofu*, Sensei," I replied.

He was sitting with a panel of judges, so he could not act freely, but I could see that he wanted to laugh. Such a reaction would have been inappropriate in a traditional Japanese martial art, during such a venue, but it was funny. I could see him trying to hold in his laughter. His lips twitched and his eyes widened. In the end, he turned to the others on the testing panel and said, "Give that boy a shodan." Then he sent me away. I never forgot this examination.

Although all martial arts tests and ranks are ultimately unimportant, beginning students have a fundamental emotional need for some sort of symbol of their dedication and development of skill or knowledge. But it is important for students to understand that rank is only a *symbol* of their accomplishments. It does not convey them. Anyone can buy a belt or title; it is vital to develop the skills that the rank should symbolize. This is an important difference, and it should be understood, if true progress is to be made in a martial discipline. "I will train hard and get rank" is the wrong attitude, because it puts the rank above the skills themselves. The desire to learn the art should be the driving force, not the desire to have rank or status within the art. Generally, the more one trains the more insignificant ranks and titles are. As long as people continue to train, they will eventually begin to understand. They will come to realize that titles are insignificant.

The great teachers I have known have never called themselves by any fancy title. For example, Aikido's founder Ueshiba Morihei was respectfully called O-Sensei by his students, but he never referred to himself by anything other than his name. The same is true for Tohei Koichi and all of the other master instructors who are recognized today for their genius and skill. It was we, their students, who call them Sensei or O-Sensei as a sign of respect for their accomplishments and time served in the art. This respect cannot be demanded. It must be given. Other than on official documents, I have never seen any of them sign a title after their names. Yet today people seemingly love to use titles. Some use terms like sensei, shihan, hanshi, kaicho, dojo-cho, and soke to refer to themselves. Such people are not only ignorant of the Japanese culture and language, but also of the very spirit of Budo that they claim to represent and teach. Shihan actually means "role model," and some of the people who call themselves by this title are anything but role models. These Japanese terms, and others like them, have precise meanings within various martial arts systems, and they were typically used or given after the rank of fifth-dan. There seems to be an obsession in the West with having some sort of exotic title that nobody really understands. Obviously, you cannot call yourself a doctor without going through particular training. Likewise, people cannot use the title sensei, soke, or kaicho when referring to themselves, without having had it bestowed upon them by others who are in a position to do so. And such terms can never be used to refer to oneself.

I have often wondered what drives this behavior. The important thing is your skill and ability, and not what you wear or what title you demand. You could call Tohei Sensei a fifth-kyu, and yet it would not affect his skill level at all. It would not reduce his martial ability. After a long time practicing the martial arts, practitioners will come to realize that they do not need outward things anymore. Such things are only an expression of ego and insecurity. The things that have meaning are the rich experiences that occur after walking the martial path for a long time. There are no shortcuts. As beginners progress, learning the techniques, they become proud and self-confident. As they continue to train, this pride vanishes, and humility takes its place. They become people who others want to emulate. Humility is not giving up anything. It is the final act of understanding what this path is really all about.

16. Michi "The Way"

CHAPTER 4:
BUDO: A MIND AND BODY CHANGING METHOD

*I*n 1960, I decided to move to the United States, where it seemed that martial arts were more popular. All of the decent Judo books (in languages other than Japanese) were in English. The first worthwhile text I found was Kyuzo Mifune's *Canon of Judo*. It helped clarify some of the things I had been practicing, and made me think a little harder about martial arts in general and Judo in particular. I arrived in the United States during the summer of 1960, found a place to live in Los Angeles, and began training at Harold Sharp's dojo. He has written many books, and has put together many videos about Judo. His teacher was ninth-dan Takahiko Ishikawa, the All-Japan Champion in 1949 and 1950.

Ishikawa conveyed his thoughts regarding how to become a Judo champion: he often "spoke of the importance of mind, posture, control, and training," all of which are interrelated. It is strange to say, but some Judo players do not really pay attention to what their teachers are saying. They will listen and nod, but when they go back to training, they continue to do things as they once had. They practice their favorite techniques repeatedly, and they never reach their full potential. Hal Sharp tried to absorb all of his teacher's suggestions, and he later wrote:

> *By following his suggestions, my power, mentally and physically, seemed to double. I rarely was thrown. I became very positive and aggressive and stopped defensive actions. I learn to take advantage of my opponent's movements. I stopped trying to force my favorite techniques on my opponent. Instead, I attacked based on the opportunity my opponent gave me.*[5]

Ishikawa Sensei believed that you had to use your mind correctly to emerge victorious. When he was young, he would prepare for championships by stating repeatedly "I am going to win." He would also mentally plan the techniques that he was going to use in matches. But as he grew older, and as he trained more, he became a much better practitioner. He still had the same confidence, but he no longer planned his techniques. Randori is not kata. Instead, he used the opponents' own actions to overcome them. This is the principle behind all great martial arts: use your opponent's own force to defeat him. By using his force, rather than extending your own energy into him, you always keep yourself in a safe position. Another important mental attribute involves discipline and willpower. It connects to shugyo, hard or ascetic training, and it can be reduced to the following expression: "never give up." An example of this determination is a match Ishikawa had against a strong opponent named Daigo during the 1949 All-Japan Championship.

Daigo attempted to perform an *uchi-mata*, an inner thigh sweep. In the performance of this technique, he crushed one of Ishikawa's testicles, and due to the injury, Ishikawa became unconscious. When he was revived, despite the pain, he continued to fight and win. After winning this match, he went on to fight Kimura, who was known as the toughest competitor in Japan. They tied in the main bout, and the first extension also ended in a draw. The head referee, Mifune, whose book I still own, decided not to have a second extension. He declared both players champions. Immediately after the bout, Ishikawa collapsed and they took him to the hospital. This dedication and mental fortitude is what separates champions from everyone else. This steadfastness is praised in the famous samurai text *Hagakure*:

It is written that the priest Shungaku said, "In just refusing to retreat from something one gains the strength of two men." This is interesting. Something that is not done at the time and at that place will remain unfinished for a lifetime. At a time when it is difficult to complete matters with the strength of a single man, one will bring it to a conclusion with the strength of two. If one thinks about it later, he will be negligent all his life. "Stamp quickly and pass through a wall of iron" is another interesting phrase. To quickly break in and step through directly is the first step of celerity.[6]

If practitioners train in the correct manner, this mental discipline should be developed just as the body is developed. This takes much more than just showing up to the dojo, working out mindlessly, and then going back to day-to-day life with no thought whatsoever of Budo. Instead, you must take what you learn at the dojo and apply it to life outside of it. Ishikawa told Hal Sharp "for every hour you train at the dojo with others, you should train two hours by yourself." Sharp listened to his teacher. He learned from him, and he passed that knowledge on to those of us who trained with him. Budo is not just in the dojo, and correct training will lead to positive changes in one's mental fortitude and physical structure.

After training in martial arts for decades, you begin to look past what someone is wearing to truly see him or her. And based on how someone moves, acts, and reacts, you can tell how advanced that person is in the martial arts. I remember an interesting occurrence that happened a couple years before moving to the United States. I was training in Basel, Switzerland: a pretty city on the Rhine River. Kondo Sensei from the Kodokan was there. It was said that he was a descendent of Kondo Isami, a member of the *Shinsengumi*, a feared group of warriors that existed until the Meiji Restoration and Commodore Perry's visit. They were responsible for assassinations and political duels in Kyoto.

Kondo certainly had the discipline attributed to samurai. His classes were intense. And he liked to do a lot of *shimewaza*, choking techniques. Before allowing people to choke others, he wanted to make sure they knew what it felt like. Therefore, he would choke us until we became unconscious and then revive us. This practice made us aware of just how dangerous such techniques were – that they were not to be taken lightly. (I would not suggest doing this, as it is dangerous!)

I eventually made it to yondan in Judo, but my nidan test was unusual and memorable. I had trained day and night to perform the lengthy kata required in the examination. When I showed up at the dojo for the test, I was prepared. Kondo asked, "What test are you taking?"

I told him, and he asked me to turn around and walk away from him, then turn and return to him. After seeing me move, he said, "You passed." I learned later that after training in the martial arts for many years, you can evaluate someone's skill by seeing the changes that have taken place in his or her body. The martial arts truly are a body and mind changing discipline.

Years later in Japan, (in 1967), I was walking along a street in Tokyo and saw a man coming toward me from the opposite direction wearing traditional garb. I knew right away that this man was a martial artist. He, in turn, recognized my friend and me as martial artists also. He introduced himself as Saito. We wanted to talk, so we stopped into a small bar to grab a couple of drinks. We told him that we were training in Aikido and that we were in Japan to train with the founder. Saito said that he was a sword instructor at a nearby dojo. Then he started pulling photos out of his kimono. In those days, there were riots at universities. To deal with the unruly crowds, the police would bring in Saito, but not how you would think. He boarded a helicopter, they flew directly over the crowd, and he climbed down a ladder into the center of the people with only a wooden sword. Then he would start swinging it, and as seen from above, the circle around him became increasingly larger. This was riot control back then.

I think I improved a lot while training at Hal Sharp's dojo. I trained with Gene LeBelle often, and he always defeated me. Such training is important in the development of a good martial artist. It cannot be bypassed. Tendo-ryu instructor Sawada Hanae (b. 1917), while speaking to one of her students, said:

> Only through losing can you understand what it means to win. But you only know about winning. You need to lose and then examine your mental state. You have to realize, "Ah, this is what it feels like to lose." Then, you must do the same thing next time you win. If you don't know what it feels like to both win and lose, then you cannot win. If you can't lose, you can't win. This is a very important thing.[7]

My time training at this dojo was formative to say the least, as it was at this time that I was introduced for the first time to the art that I would study for the rest of my life: Aikido. I will never forget the day that I saw Ueshiba Kisshomaru's demonstration. I remember seeing people fly through the air in ways that Judo people do not take ukemi. It all seemed so effortless. There was no pushing or pulling, as I often saw in Judo matches. It looked instead like the attackers were throwing themselves. Based on my limited understanding of martial arts, I thought they must have been throwing themselves. Certainly, no one could throw others around so effortlessly. That is why I challenged him during the question-and-answer session. After he injured my wrists I understood that there was something real to this art. There was something powerful that I wished to explore. I trained with him while he was in the United States, and when he returned to Japan I began training with Takahashi Isao, who taught me much about the art called Aikido, in addition to Zen Buddhism, Japanese calligraphy, and swords.

17. Kenko: The Glint of a Sword

CHAPTER 5:
A LESSON FROM TAKAHASHI ISAO

*T*akahashi Isao (1912-1972) lived in Japan until he was ten years old, then moved to Hawaii, where he trained with Tohei Koichi for many years. He became a seventh-dan in Aikido, and also achieved high ranks in both Judo and Kendo. He always had great insights into the martial arts, and constantly explained things in a clear manner. Zen influenced him and he practiced Zen-related arts like calligraphy. He was also interested in swords and the tea ceremony. In 1960, he moved to Los Angeles and became the chief instructor of the Los Angeles Aikikai. That is where I first met him.

18. Takahashi Isao demonstrating irimi-nage. I am uke. (1962).

19. Takashi Sensei (center), Kobayashi Sensei (second to left, seated), Me (far right, seated) right after the full tea cup lesson.

When I first started training with Takahashi Sensei, I was still confident in my skills. Despite my wake-up calls in France, being thrown on the street and in the dojo, and being tossed around by someone whom I had planned to use for warm-up practice, I was confident in my abilities. This, in and of itself, is probably a good thing, but I was still lacking humility. I was confident in my sword skills. I was president of the Japanese Sword Society, and I also trained in Kendo with Miyahara Maki and Mori Torao. Mori Sensei was a strong influence. I thought he was one of the best swordsmen alive; at least, he was the best with whom I had ever had the pleasure of training. One time, I saw him in an incredible match. His opponent knocked the shinai out of his hands. Like most observers, I assumed that the match was over and that he had lost. But without a second's hesitation, he pulled off his left *kote* (protector) with his right hand, as if drawing a sword, and flung it at the opponent. The reaction was natural and spontaneous, and it took the opponent by surprise. He tried to avoid it. As he moved out the way, Mori Sensei swiftly moved in and threw him with *osoto-gari*. It was one of the most natural and spontaneous reactions I had ever seen.

20. A picture of me when I was president of the Japanese Sword Society. The scroll behind me was penned by the legendary swordsman Tesshu Yamaoka.

Another time, we were in my living room drinking tea. We were sitting around a low, red lacquered table. I am fond of the table, and I would hate if anything ever happened to it. Mori Sensei and I were talking about swords and swordsmanship, and I was trying to understand how precise swordsmen actually needed to be. I wanted to know how precise a sword could be. After some discussion, Mori Sensei shook his head and cleared the table, removing our teacups and a book or two that might have been on its surface. He laid a Los Angeles telephone book on it, and I watched in horror as he calmly drew his sword and cut the book in half. I looked at what he had done. The book was cut perfectly, two clean-edged halves. Worried about my precious table, I push the pieces aside to inspect the damage. There was none. There was not a single mark on the table. Mori Sensei looked at me and smiled. "You should be that precise," he said, "every time."

The fact that Mori Sensei was my teacher made my think that my skills were also superb. Of course, this reasoning does not make much sense, but like all martial artists, no matter which martial art they study, I was still learning. I was full of myself. Takahashi Sensei was a well-known Aikido instructor, but assuredly, he was no match for me with a sword! That is truly what I thought at the time. I bragged to him that I knew how to handle a Japanese sword. I told him that, someday, I would like to "try him out."

He responded, "How about now?" And he did not even bother to pick up a shinai. Instead, he grabbed a broom that he had laying around the dojo. I picked up my weapon and squared off with him. I was confident that I would emerge victorious, and I considered how callous it was of Takahashi Sensei to have misjudged my skill. He lowered the broom into *gedan* position. He did not provide any openings where I could strike. I recognized that despite his seemingly inferior position, he had the advantage. He took a step forward, closing the distance between us, and I sensed that I was in trouble. I stepped backward. This same occurrence, with minor variations alone, happened many times, until I finally realized that I was no match for him. I bowed and expressed my sentiments. He smiled and nodded.

Funakoshi Gichin described the same type of situation, in which a competition was decided without actually having a match, but with much graver possibilities; it was a match that would determine the life or death of the competitors.[8] One of Funakoshi's teachers was Master Matsumura, who walked into an engraver's shop in Naha, Okinawa, hoping to have a design put onto a pipe. The engraver was also an accomplished martial artist, and he asked, "Aren't you Matsumura, the famous karate teacher?"

"Yes," he replied. "Why?"

"Well, I was hoping that I could train with you."

Matsumura shook his head, saying, "I do not teach anymore. Besides, why should someone like yourself, who is also known as an expert, want to train with me?"

"To tell you the truth," the engraver said, "I am curious to see how you teach."

"I already told you," Matsumura replied, "I no longer teach."

21. Takahashi Sensei (center), (c. 1964) Meik Skoss and Bill Erbeck are in the back row, I am front right, seated. The girl to the left of Sensei is Kuki (Miriam) Lambert, the most advanced female student in our dojo at that time.

The engraver then turned serious, and his tone of voice became less friendly. "In that case, would you have a match with me?"

Matsumura was incredulous, and he explained that a match was serious. It was a matter of life and death. He said, "I know that you are skilled at karate, but are you willing to die?"

"I am ready to die," he responded.

"Then I will oblige you," Matsumura said. "Of course, there is an old saying that we should remember: when two tigers fight, one is bound to be killed, the other maimed. Let me know where and when, and I will be there."

The engraver suggested that they meet at 5:00 the next morning in the Kimbu graveyard, behind Tama Palace. They arrived and squared off. The engraver made the first move, taking a lower posture and closing the distance between them. Despite the engraver's movements, and his adoption of a fighting stance, Matsumura did not budge. He did not react at all. Thinking that he had no way to defend himself, the engraver initiated an attack. At that moment, Matsumura stared at his opponent, and a force that seemed to emanate from the karate master's eyes repelled the engraver. He took a step backward, attempting to regain his nerve. He was sweating, and he could feel his heart beating quickly. He sat down on a nearby rock, not understanding what had occurred. Matsumura then called out, "Come on. Let's get on with it."

The engraver stood up and, once again, adopted a fighting stance. Matsumura remained in a natural stance. As before, the engraver closed the distance and attempted an attack, but once again, an unseen force repelled him. He did not understand what was happening, and he did not know what to do, but he was determined to win. He would rather die than lose the match. He shouted, a loud *kiai* that shook the cemetery and echoed into the distance, but Matsumura did not react at all. He waited, and then Matsumura let out a loud *kiai*. The engraver felt it. It affected him and he could not move. He fell to the ground, saying, "I give up. I was foolish to challenge you. Your skills are superb and I am no match for you."

Matsumura said, "You are wrong. Your skills are formidable, and if we had actually exchanged blows I may have lost."

The engraver shook his head. "I don't think so. I felt completely helpless. I was so frightened by your eyes that I lost the desire to fight."

"Maybe," Matsumura said, "but there was an important difference between us: you were determined to win, but I was determined to die if I lost. This mindset makes the difference."

This is a famous story that is continually repeated to teach practitioners of karate or other martial arts an important lesson. Wherever you see versions of the story, the dialogs might be a bit different, but the underlying event is the same. Many martial art legends that are passed down as historical might not be. On the other hand, they might be historical yet exaggerated. This is a common human tendency. Historical people who many admire gain almost superhuman attributes as time progresses. However, the stories are passed down to teach an important lesson. In this particular one, Matsumura's skill had transcended physical techniques. There was something else going on, perhaps something spiritual. He had an ocular power that was palpable, a power that could be used to affect others.

The belief in an eye power that can influence others is found all over the world, from notions of the evil-eye, called *isabat al-'ayn* in Arabic, *olho gordo* in Portuguese, *malocchio* in Italian, and *μάτι* (*mati*) in Greek, to the Japanese classifications of different eye-powers under the more general headings of *metsuke* and *kihaku*. Metsuke literally means "attaching the eyes," but usually refers to how to use the eyes and where to fix the eyes in combat. (Proper metsuke allows one to read his or her opponent's intent, and to be aware of the environment.) However, there seems to be other types of eye power. One of them is perceived as a power emanating from the eyes that can halt an attacker. This power is called *kihaku*. To avoid the effects of this power, some martial disciplines specifically teach their students to avoid eye contact.

O-Sensei warned his students: "Do not stare into the eyes of your opponent: He may mesmerize you." In Aikido, practitioners might not gain a true understanding of the founder's words, as students do not tend to stare into their opponents' eyes. The concept of influencing an opponent through eye contact is most likely not understood by many martial artists in general, never mind Aikido practitioners. A true assessment of Ueshiba's statement, however, might make a student ask, "How can one mesmerize an opponent, only by looking into his eyes?" Ueshiba warned his students not to look into the eyes of an opponent, as they could be transfixed, possibly controlled. It is probable that he knew this from personal experience, as it is (likely) not only a technique that he experienced, but one that he also possessed. Many who knew him personally can confirm that he had "piercing eyes."

His son, Ueshiba Kisshomaru, wrote, *"The founder had a powerful effect not just on those direct students who he instructed every day but even on people simply watching his demonstrations or observing classes at the dojo: they said his eyes glittered with a penetration that could pierce metal."* O-Sensei was not unique in this regard; there are reports of many other masters, from diverse martial arts, who (seemingly) possessed the power to control opponents through eye contact alone. What this power is, and how it is developed, is generally unknown.

Even experiencing it seems to be a rarity. However, there are individuals alive today, who have studied martial disciplines for an extended period, who possess this unusual skill. Unraveling such mysterious skills takes serious study and discipline. Students who just come by the dojo, train, and then go home, without giving the underlying significance of the art's principles a second thought will never come to understand such high-level techniques. Martial studies should not cease once the physical motions alone have been mastered. There is much more to the martial arts, many layers of mysteries. To unravel those layers takes years of wholehearted practice.

Back to the famous karate tale: besides this eye power, Matsumura described the mindset that determined victory: he was willing to die if he lost. This frame of mind does not automatically develop on its own through the rote training of physical techniques. Rather, serious martial art practitioners must make the choice to develop this mindset, and it will only come about through serious discipline and training: shugyo. Everyone goes through the same stages in martial art development. They are never bypassed. At first, you might look at high-ranking masters and think that there is no way that you can attain what they have attained, but if you keep training and do not give up, you will eventually approach their skill. However, this takes time and dedication. It also takes the right mental outlook and discipline, which is why many students of the martial arts also train in Zen.

22. Mushin (No Mind)

CHAPTER 6:
ZEN IN THE MARTIAL ARTS

*B*uddhism began in the fifth or sixth century B.C.E. with the enlightenment of Siddhartha Gautama, otherwise known as Sakyamuni, or Sage of the Sakya Clan. After engaging in extreme ascetic practices for years, he became the Buddha, or Enlightened One, while meditating under a tree at Bodh Gaya. Immediately after his enlightenment, he spent several weeks in the same area assimilating all of the knowledge and understanding that he had acquired. Then he began teaching others about the Four Noble Truths and the Noble Eightfold Path. The Buddha used something called expedient means to instruct his followers. He altered the substantive nature of his sermons based on the listeners present, so at times, it might have seemed that paradoxical information was conveyed. However, he was behaving like a doctor. Just as a good doctor would not give the same medication to all of his patients, the Buddha conveyed different information based upon his audiences' needs. For this reason, some diverse beliefs are found among Buddhists, and when Buddhism merged with pre-existing religious faiths, sects developed. Buddhism was introduced to China in the first century C.E. It was there that Ch'an (Zen) Buddhism later developed.

Some believe that Zen originated with what is today known as the Flower Sermon. A crowd had gathered to listen to the Buddha, but he did not talk. Instead, he held up a flower. Only one person in the audience, Mahakasyapa, understood the significance of this, and upon receiving the knowledge bestowed upon him by the Buddha, he smiled. This is a direct transmission of knowledge without reliance upon words. Certainly, this does seem in tune with Zen teachings. Traditionally, the following story explains Zen's origin: In the fifth century, an Indian monk named Bodhidharma traveled to China, carrying the Buddha's teachings. Supposedly, Emperor Wu met with him. He considered himself Buddhist and had constructed numerous temples. He had also overseen the translation of various religious sutras, and he gave a great deal of money to the *sangha*, the monks and nuns who studied in the temples he had erected. He supposedly asked Bodhidharma, "What is the merit that I have accrued by doing such great works?"

Bodhidharma replied, "None at all, your Majesty."

The Emperor did not understand his reply and was offended. However, the response exemplified the Buddhist doctrine of emptiness. Bodhidharma left the royal palace and headed toward Shaolin Temple. He is the legendary founder of Shaolin Kung Fu, as he allegedly taught the monks breathing techniques and physical exercises. This runs contrary to another activity that is attributed to him: upon arriving, he purportedly meditated in a cave near the temple for nine years. It has been said that he cut off his eyelids to prevent falling asleep. Supposedly, he meditated for so long that his arms and legs stopped functioning. (In Japan, Bodhidharma is known as Daruma, and it is for this reason that daruma dolls have no arms and no legs.) If this story were taken literally, it would make the transmission of physical exercises impossible. Everything surrounding this person is legendary, and such stories should not be taken literally and thought of in a historical sense. Such tales have been added to possible historic events to teach important concepts. According to the legends, when he exited the cave after nine years, he began teaching the monks who resided at the nearby temple. His teachings became known as Ch'an Buddhism, which is from the Sanskrit word *dhyana*, meaning "meditation." In Japan, Ch'an became Zen.

23. Statue of Amida Buddha at Kamakura, Japan.

In the twelfth century, Eisai Myoan traveled to China to study Buddhism. He returned, hoping to establish Zen Buddhism in his home country. It did not last. Later, Nanpo Shomyo (1235–1308) also traveled to China to learn Ch'an. When he returned, he taught the Japanese. He founded the Rinzai sect. In 1215, Dogen traveled to China, and upon his return, he established the Soto sect. Some Chinese priests and their Japanese students who were living in Uji established the Obaku Zen Buddhist sect in 1661. These three sects are still extant in Japan. Soto has the most adherents, Obaku the fewest. Rinzai attracted the interest of many martial artists due to some of the sect's practices. One of them seems harsh: while monks are meditating, their teacher will come up behind them and strike them with a wooden board called *kyosaku*. The following is a famous Rinzai Zen story:

A student asked the master a question, and the teacher replied, "I am not wise enough to answer that question." He pointed at a mountain in the distance. "However, if you climb that mountain, a master there can answer it." Right away, the student set out to meet the master and find the answer to his question. He was gone for days. Eventually, he returned and approached his teacher. He said, "Master, I climbed the mountain, found the teacher, and asked him the question. All he did was hit me with a stick."

The master replied, "He did? Oh, what a kind and gentle man!"

Rinzai Zen tales, which include violent references, do not just involve the kyosaku. The following is a Ch'an tale from China:

Kuei-shan Ling-yu once said, "Many masters have acquired insight regarding the Great Body, but they do not know anything about Great Use."

One of his disciples, Yang-shan, repeated this to a monk living in a humble mountain dwelling. Then he asked, "What do you think about Kuei-shan?"

The monk asked him to repeat what he had said. When Yang-shan began speaking, the monk kicked him so hard that he fell to the ground. He got up and, nursing his injury, returned to his master, to whom he explained what had occurred. When Kuei-shan heard the story, he laughed aloud.

References to Zen masters hitting students relate to something often heard in dojo. When students are talking too much instead of training, teachers might say, "Shut up and train!" This statement, in a sense, sums up a philosophy inherent in Rinzai Zen. It emphasizes *kensho*, finding one's true nature, and adherents believe that this can never be found in words. It must be experienced directly, like the Buddha's Flower Sermon, in which the teaching was conveyed directly. It was delivered before an entire audience of people, yet only one among them was able to discern the intended meaning. This discernment is developed in Rinzai Zen through seated meditation and *samu*: physical work that is done with complete focus. *Koan* are also used. These seemingly illogical questions cannot be answered with the rational mind. One example is "What is the sound of one hand clapping?" Another is "What was the appearance of your face before your ancestors were born?" The idea behind such unusual questions is to shut off the rational mind, to free oneself of all thoughts, so that the mind can become open and free. It is only in this state that it can absorb anything significant. It is only in the state that enlightenment can occur.

All Zen practitioners strive to understand the essence of the universe through direct experience. While other Buddhist sects focus on scriptures and pray to various Buddhas and Bodhisattvas, Zen emphasizes training to develop insight into the true nature of one's own mind, to reveal one's own inner Buddha nature. A famous story illustrates this self-reliance:

A monk lived alone in a small hut and spent his days in quiet meditation, seeking enlightenment. Someone gave him a small statue of Buddha, and he brought it back to his hut. He said to the statue, "My home is very small Mr. Buddha, but I will share it with you. But please do not think that I am asking you for help. I will attain enlightenment on my own."

To accomplish this, many practitioners train in *zazen*, which means, "seated Zen." This practice might appear simple, but like the martial arts, it takes years to become proficient. First, practitioners learn how to sit correctly, with the body in the correct position. Then, they are taught to concentrate on the breath. This has nothing to do with meditation, but it is a means of pointing people in the correct direction. They must learn to control their thoughts. For most people, the mind is restless, and they have to practice for months before they are able to control it. Eventually, meditators become inwardly calm, and they attain "the original mind," which is free and spacious, like wind passing through the open sky. Thoughts might appear, but they just float by. They disappear just as they appeared, leaving no trace at all. Eventually, practitioners hope to achieve insight into the true nature of the universe.

The state of mind developed through Zen meditation is beneficial to the martial arts. When the mind is calm, actions are natural and spontaneous. It is for this reason that warriors in medieval Japan trained in Zen not to become spiritually enlightened, but to become better fighters. It is a paradoxical concept, but the more one studies martial arts the more one perceives a spiritual element. Likewise, the more one trains in Zen, the more skilled he or she becomes in the arts of war. Concepts such as *zanshin* (remaining mind) and

**24. Fujiwara no Hidesato demonstrating Zanshin.
Woodblock print by Tsukioka Yoshitoshi (1890).**

mushin (no mind), which are heard in martial arts dojo all over the world, originated in the Zen tradition.

These two concepts are related, and they are difficult to define. In some martial arts, the idea of the remaining mind is taken literally. In Kyudo, for example, the Japanese art of archery, zanshin is one's remaining attention after the arrow has been let go. Although the string of the bow had been released and the arrow flew toward its target, the mind continues to maintain its concentration; it remains focused.

Zanshin also involves constant awareness, so it is not good if people are so completely engrossed in their activities that they cannot sense potential danger. It is remaining focused on an action, yet being completely aware of one's surroundings. In Zen, meditation is not just being completely absorbed in one's own breathing and the way he or she is sitting. Concentration on the breath, which will later lead to true meditation, is important, but the meditator must remain aware of his or her surroundings.

Mushin translates as no-mind, but it refers to a mind that is empty of thoughts yet maintains complete concentration. A basic example of this concept is the following: Judo practitioners might practice *kuzushi*, unbalancing their partners, hundreds of times. Then, they practice *tsukuri*, fitting in, repeatedly. Finally, they blend these two actions and then throw the opponent. At first, beginners struggle with these movements. It is not easy to take someone's balance. In time, provided they are dedicated and constantly practice, they find it increasingly easier to play with someone's balance to gain the advantage. When they practice fitting in, it is initially difficult to keep their partners off-balance throughout the process. But slowly, they learn to time this movement so that a throw can be executed before their partners regain their footing. This is not an easy process. It cannot be rushed, and if students do not practice their hearts out, they will never be skillful. However, after years of practice, they are able to blend these movements together so that there is no thought whatsoever of them being separate. They are the same. Eventually, this is taken a step further, and various techniques are executed without conscious thought. This is an example of mushin.

When I was still competing in Judo, early in my Aikido career, I experienced mushin. I like to tell people that I lost my mind, as that is close to what the term actually means in Japanese. When I faced a difficult opponent, I made every effort to clear my mind and simply do the best techniques possible. One time I stepped onto the mat and attempted to do the same thing; I cleared my mind of all thoughts. This time, however, everything went away. And I mean *everything*: the crowd, the noise, the feel of the mat under my feet, my opponent, even myself. Everything was gone. I finally came back to the world when my opponent hit the mat and the judge yelled, "Point!"

All four judges immediately began to argue about which technique I had just used. One of them turned toward me and asked, "What did you do? What technique was that?"

I had no idea, and in those days, before video recording, instant replay was not an option. Everyone had a different opinion as to what had just occurred, including the judges, the crowd, and even the opponent. I still do not know exactly what happened. All I knew then, and all I know now, is that for a moment, I was not there, and yet the same time, I was more completely aware than I ever had been before. In a sense, it was as though I had ceased to exist. The only thing that existed was the technique, which expressed itself through me. This feeling is difficult to convey to others, and to understand fully, it must be experienced. This will only happen through shugyo. Since then, it has happened numerous other times. The sense of self disappears, and techniques flow through me on their own accord. But that time on the Judo mat was the first clear memory I have of it.

We often talk of mushin and no mind, and there are many ideas and accounts of what it might be like, or what it should be like, but this is just an intellectual activity for most people. Such accounts are helpful in that they point individuals in the right direction, but experience alone is the key to understanding. Attempting to understand something intellectually first and then trying to experience it is the wrong way of thinking. If students think in this manner, they will not progress.

The martial arts have many layers, and studying Zen can help them to discover meaning. Zen can improve their martial abilities, and the martial arts can help them to live better lives. This connection has been explored for hundreds of years. One only needs to look at the writings of Takuan Soho (1573-1645) to understand this. Takuan was a follower of the Rinzai sect of Zen. He was not a martial artist, yet many famous martial artists turned to him for assistance. He wrote the *Mysterious Record of Immovable Wisdom* for swordsman

Yagyu Munenori, the *Clear Sound of Jewels* for Musashi Miyamoto, and it is possible that he wrote the *Annals of the Sword Taia* for Ono Tadaaki. (It might have been written instead for Yagyu Munenori; it is uncertain.) Sword masters turned to a Zen monk for help in wielding the sword, a person who had never wielded a sword. This is profound, and many martial insights, including where to fix the eyes in combat and where to keep the mind, stem from this Zen priest's teachings.

Regarding where to place the eyes in combat, he offered this suggestion:

> When facing a single tree, if you look at a single one of its red leaves, you will not see all the others. When the eye is not set on any one leaf, and you face the tree with nothing at all in mind, any number of leaves is visible to the eye without limit. But if a single leaf holds the eye, it will be as if the remaining leaves were not there.[10]

I think this is the most logical analogy when thinking about where to keep the eyes in combat. You must train so that you do not miss the entire tree while focusing on one leaf alone. You must learn to perceive the one leaf, and all of the other leaves and the tree at the same time. His advice regarding where to place the mind in combat is just as wise, as relevant today as it was in the 1600s when he taught Yagyu:

> If you put [your mind] in your right hand, it will be taken by the right hand and your body will lack its functioning. If you put your mind in the eye, it will be taken by the eye, and your body will lack its functioning. If you put your mind in your right foot, your mind will be taken by the right foot, and your body will lack its functioning. No matter where you put it, if you put the mind in one place, the rest of the body will lack its functioning. If you don't put it anywhere, it will go to all parts of your body and extend throughout its entirety.[11]

This is a great explanation for the importance of mushin, but these are just cursory examples of the profound connection between Zen and the martial arts. Specific Zen concepts can be continually analyzed and applied to martial strategy, but the connection between physical techniques and spirituality is deeper. When training in the martial arts, practitioners follow a path. Think of it like a path up a mountain. At the beginning, they set out on the path, learning basic stances and techniques, but the summit is not visible. As they continue training, they become increasingly more skillful. They are progressing further along the path, yet the summit is still not visible. As long as they continue their training, the physical techniques become a doorway into a spiritual dimension, and as they begin to explore this connection, the misty clouds drift away, revealing the mountaintop. They can then forge through and stand at the summit.

At this point, others look at such practitioners as masters. But the masters themselves know that their trip is not yet over. They continue down, over the other side of the mountain, following unknown paths, which will lead them back home. Eventually, they return to where they had started. They might look the same, but they are not. They have changed. On one level, the Zen circle, called *enso,* illustrates this principle. The journey is circular, and eventually, the traveler will end up where he or she started. This Zen story illustrates the same principle:

A monk leaves his home and goes in search of enlightenment. He travels to distant lands, learning about diverse cultures. He piles experience upon experience, yet does not come any closer to enlightenment. Eventually he gives up and returns home. Upon arriving, he is awakened to the true principles of the universe. Enlightenment occurs. He says, "I have traveled to distant places, searching for something that has been here, with me, the entire time. It would've been better to have been deaf, dumb, and blind from the very beginning."

Zen makes use of ox-herding pictures to illustrate the same type of journey: the natural progression that occurs through hard training (shugyo). The pictures metaphorically illustrate stages along the path. The first picture shows the ox herder looking for the ox (his true nature). In the next one, he finds tracks and follows them, and he is now amazed that he ever missed them in the first place. "Along the riverbank, and under the trees, I discover footprints!

Even under the fragrant grass, I see his prints. Deep in remote mountains, they are found. These traces no more can be hidden than one's nose looking heavenward."[12] In the third picture, he sees the ox. Fourth, he struggles to tame it. Fifth, he is successful. He tames it, and it becomes naturally gentle. Unfettered, it obeys the ox herder. In the sixth picture, the herder rides the ox home, playing songs of profound meaning on his flute. Seventh, he arrives home, and the ox disappears. In the eighth illustration, both the ox and the individual have transcended reality. "Whip, rope, person and bull – all merge in no-thing. This heaven is so vast no message can stain it. How may a snowflake exist in a raging fire? Here are the footprints of the patriarchs."[13] In the ninth picture, the herder returns to the source, and in the tenth and final picture, he returns to normal human society. He is happy and ready to help others.

25. Searching for the Ox

26. Discovering Footprints

27. Perceiving the Ox

28. Catching the Ox

29. Taming the Ox

30. Riding the Ox home

31. The Ox transcends

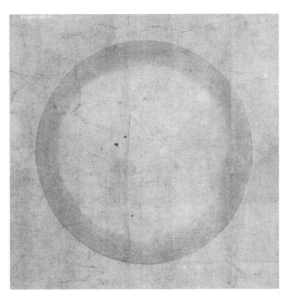

32. Both Ox and Self transcend

33. Returning to the Source

34. Returning to the World

All serious martial arts practitioners should consider these stages. They cannot be bypassed. Many great martial artists turn to religion or other spiritual disciplines to complete their training. This combination of the martial and spiritual paths makes them great. O-Sensei, the founder of Aikido, trained in Daito-ryu Aikijujutsu. Then he began teaching this art. Later, he studied the religious teachings of Omoto-kyo. Aikido was created when he joined these two paths. The lessons learned in the dojo should carry over into life outside the training facility. In this way, Zen helps to establish dojo lessons as veritable life lessons. Zen has also strongly influenced other Japanese arts, such as painting, calligraphy and the tea ceremony.

35. Enso, The Zen Circle

CHAPTER 7:
ZEN CALLIGRAPHY AND ITS CONNECTION TO MARTIAL ARTS

I have been interested in all things Japanese since I was a child. I read every book I could find on Japanese art, and started *sumi-e* (Japanese ink painting) and *shodo* (Japanese calligraphy) at about the same time I began training in the martial arts. I also started studying Zen at about the same period as well. Shodo and Sumi-e are both Zen art forms, and for me, they are more effective than seated meditation. While sitting, it is easy for the mind to move about, but as soon as I place a brush in my hand, I attain a state of total focus. I become completely focused on the task at hand. This is Zen. A monk once said the following to a famous Zen master, Joshu: "I have just entered the monastery. Please tell me what to do."

Joshu responded, "Have you eaten yet?"

"Yes, I have," the monk replied.

"Then you had better wash your bowl."

It is said that the monk attained enlightenment upon hearing these words. This teaching indicates that one should be here and now, in the present, without distracting thoughts. Another parable is used to illustrate the same concept:

The Zen monks Tanzan Hara (1819-1892) and Ekido Zenji were walking along a road after a great storm and they noticed a young woman in a pretty *kimono* trying to cross a stream. The water was much higher than normal and there was no way that she could possibly cross without dirtying her clothing. Tanzan offered his assistance. He picked her up and carried her to the other side. She thanked him and they went their separate ways. The monks continued walking. After several miles, Ekido stopped, turned to Tanzan, and asked, "How could you have picked up that woman back there? It is against our sect's rules to touch a woman."

Tanzan replied, "I set that woman down some time ago. Why are you still carrying her?"

Although this story is historical, other similar parables might not be. As previously mentioned, sometimes fictional stories are added to the biographies of famous people to teach a profound lesson. Some human beings, in time, became thought of as deities, which might be an inadvertent consequence of such additions. However, such additions serve a purpose. They are important. These Zen parables, involving the monk who needs to focus on the task at hand and wash his bowl, and the other who needs to keep his mind in the present and forget the girl he had recently seen, teaches a Zen truth. One must remain firmly in the present, completely engaged in the current activity. This mindset encompasses both zanshin and mushin, and it cannot be expressed in words. It must be experienced firsthand.

Many have described Aikido as moving Zen, and for some people, it is. So is calligraphy and Sumi-e. My friend John Stevens explains this:

> The word zensho, Zen calligraphy, is of recent origin. The classical term is bokuseki, traces of ink. It is usually associated with the calligraphy of medieval Chinese and Japanese Zen priests. Such Zen calligraphy can be classified into nine groups:
>
> Inkajo, certificate of enlightenment
>
> Jigo, name given to a monk by his master
>
> Hogo, dharma talks
>
> Geju, gatha (a type of Buddhist verse)
>
> Yuige, death verse
>
> Shidogo, exhortory sermon
>
> Shi, poetry
>
> Gakuji, two or three large characters written horizontally for display on the wall or over a doorway
>
> Shokan, letters
>
> To this should be added:

San, inscriptions on Zen paintings

Ichi (ni) gyo mono, one- or two-line Zen sayings mounted on a scroll

Enso, Zen circles

However, it is done, such classification merely describes the various kinds of writing the Zen master was required to do while giving religious instruction. In themselves, these pieces cannot qualify as Zen calligraphy; they must be written in the Zen spirit. This is the criterion for zensho. Calligraphy is indeed a painting of the mind; the degree of enlightenment is expressed in the flow of the ink. Once someone mistakenly tried to efface some characters written by Wang Xizhi. He discovered that the characters had actually penetrated the wood. Regardless of how deeply he cut, it was impossible to erase them. Recently, studies by Terayama Katsujo have shown that Zen calligraphy is truly "alive." He collected authentic Zen calligraphy, forgeries of those works, and copies made by modern calligraphers and examined them with an electron microscope, magnifying certain sections from fifty to one hundred thousand times. The magnified ink particles of the authentic pieces were vibrant, full of ki, numinous; by contrast, the ink particles of the forgeries and copies were dispersed, weak, dead.[14]

To perform Zen calligraphy properly, one must abandon himself or herself in the work itself. Each piece is unique, reflecting the unique circumstances in which it was created. The calligrapher's frame of mind, the environment that surrounds the artist, the writing instrument, and the type of ink itself makes each piece unique. In the martial arts, each engagement is unique. One technique performed today should not be the same as the same technique performed tomorrow. Aikido's founder said, "The techniques of the Way of Peace change constantly; every encounter is unique, and the appropriate response should emerge naturally. Today's techniques will be different tomorrow. Do not get caught up with the form and appearance of a challenge. The Art of Peace has no form – it is the study of the spirit." Likewise, each calligraphic piece should be unique. Art forms like Japanese calligraphy and Sumi-e paintings are means of expressing the mindset acquired through Zen. Beyond that, they are ways to experience Zen. Aikido can serve the same purpose. Thinking of it in this manner, there is no difference between calligraphy, painting, the tea ceremony, Aikido, and any other martial art, if such arts are approached with the correct mental attitude.

Takahashi Sensei was inspirational in my study of Japanese calligraphy. He was a great artist himself, and I still have numerous pieces that he brushed for me. Tohei Sensei also penned calligraphy for me. I also received some instruction from Tanahashi Sensei. When I first began studying this art form, not many other people were interested in it, but for some reason, it intrigued me, so I continued my studies. Since then, I have literally sold thousands of pieces, and they are now found in collections all over the world. I work mostly in sumi and transparent watercolors, and they typically follow the tradition of *zenga* and the great masters of Zen calligraphy. I usually sign my pieces with my Buddhist name *Sando*, which means "Mountain Path," or "Mountain Way." It was given to me by a Buddhist priest named Reverend Hara when I became a lay monk in 1968, (after ten years of training). The most important thing in my artwork is to express the great principles of Zen, Aikido, and the Middle Way, as expressed by Siddhartha Gautama, the Buddha.

The historical Buddha was a wealthy prince. He gave up all his wealth and his political power to pursue ascetic training. In ancient times, people gave up many things in pursuit of the Way. This was especially true in martial studies. Today, many people think about learning a martial art and ask, "What will I gain?" Originally, it was more about "What will I lose?" Potential students literally had to abandon the lives that they knew to pursue the arts wholeheartedly. The Buddha gave up all of his riches and honors to learn about the Way. A student supposedly cut off his own left arm to study under Bodhidharma, who is considered the founder of Shaolin Kung Fu. The founder of Aikido, Ueshiba Morihei, likewise abandoned his responsibilities in northern Japan to train with the Daito-ryu genius Takeda Sokaku. My wife and I sold our house in California, so I could train with the founder for the last two years of his life.

In a real sense, the correct study of a martial art, like any spiritual discipline, is loss, not gain. A famous Zen Master once said, "To study the self is to forget the self. To forget the self is to understand all things." Another once told his student to meditate upon nothingness. After years, the student returned to the master and said, "I have finally achieved nothingness. What should I do now?"

The teacher responded, "Throw it away."

With these words, the student attained enlightenment. This mindset is sought in various disciplines. The idea of the remaining mind, no mind, and other mindsets associated with Zen are sought in Aikido, Shodo, and Sumi-e: all Zen disciplines if approached in the correct manner. This is how calligraphy is connected to Aikido:

In Aikido, we practice most *waza* (techniques) in a kata form until we learn to apply those waza in a fluid and spontaneous manner, such as in randori or a self-defense situation. Consider the benefits of kata training: in Japan and China, it is traditionally acknowledged that kata training teaches real application. The better your form is, the better your techniques are when actually applied. Some instructors believe that kata or stylized forms cannot be used in real self-defense. Kata instruction is a tradition that used to be cloaked in secrecy. The forms represent the classical vehicles through which the secrets of an art were transmitted over untold generations. In the past, this cloak was pulled even tighter. The esoteric aspects of the martial arts were kept secret from the public (and Westerners in particular) so that those in the upper ranks could maintain their authoritative positions. As a result, many instructors form their opinions of kata training based upon an incomplete understanding. Kata, or abstract forms, were intended as both a moving in-struction manual and a mnemonic aid to reveal the underlying principles of an art through practice.

Kata forms are the only reason that Aikido, as an art form, exist today. Cultural themes run through many Japanese traditions, alluding to principles and codes of conduct that seem abstract to the Western mind, but are perfect-ly natural to the Japanese. Understanding the culture of these traditions may serve to uncover the treasure buried in our own forms. I would like to expand upon this idea, using the art of calligraphy to clarify it for readers:

Shodo is the Japanese word for calligraphy, and like the word Aikido, it does not simply describe the activity, but also the philosophy that underpins it.

The term Shodo implies that mastery exists, not at the destination of a journey, but through the collective experience encountered as part of the journey. Therefore, Shodo and Aikido would translate for us as "the way or path of writing," and "the way or path of Aiki."

In China and Japan, Shodo has long been regarded as one of the most important art forms. Shodo is a hieroglyphic representation in which messages are conveyed not by individual letters, but by ideographs. Written with a brush and ground ink, the combination of complex, elegant characters and the frame of mind of the calligrapher change every character into an act of profound expression. Shodo is the dynamic execution of lines in a vast range of rhythmic combinations. The infinitely variable balance of strokes, flow and tension, and the strength and proportion of each character are the unique product of the form, artist's personality, and even the moment in time. Through Shodo, the language, eyes, and hand are linked to the deeper aspects of consciousness. This beautifully relates to kata training. An early student of O-Sensei, Shirata Rinjiro (1912–1993) explained this:

> [O-Sensei] told us that Aikido originally had no forms. The movements of the body in response to one's state of mind become the techniques. He said, "There are no techniques. What you express each time is a technique." It is the same with calligraphy. The calligraphy one produces as a beginner and the calligraphy of one's later years are different. The work is different. So you can't say which is the "true" work. As one reaches his later years, a person can express a state of absolute mental freedom through calligraphy, or any such thing. It is a way of expressing one's mind. It's a "form." The mind gradually grows and as it grows there emerges a form, a way of expression.[34]

There are many styles and forms in Shodo, ranging from rigid precision to beautiful and graceful flowing smoothness. The first definable level in Shodo is kaisho, like printing or a basic form of writing. Kaisho is the standard script, well balanced and devoid of individuality. This script displays a rigid, angular and well-defined structure. When first learning a form, Kaisho is a suitable metaphor for describing its performance. Movements are angular, well defined and devoid of rhythm. Hidden movements are abstracted, or in the case of the beginner or lazy student, not yet discovered. Such a form may claim ability and understanding, but to a master's eye, it is apparent that it is a basic, primary level. A beginner will be expected to have understood this level before he can move on.

The next level of performance is gyosho, a semi-cursive style of writing. It is a more informal way of writing, in which characters are joined together using individual, intermediate strokes. Comparing the art of calligraphy to the physical techniques in a martial art, gyosho may be considered having memorized the movements of a waza. Confidence in performing the form will free you slightly from geometrical impositions, while still adhering to the correct form. In Aikido, we call this *kihon waza*. Your awareness of the individual waza or strokes gives you more fluency from one moment to the next, and allows for some degree of individuality. Thus, you begin to understand total awareness (zanshin), in which we concentrate not only on the present (*sen*), but also on our anticipation of what follows the present (*sen no sen*).

The third style or level is sosho. It is cursive. It has no sharp angles and flows easily from character to character. Although it is an individualized and free style, there are definite rules as to what is correct and what is not. It is sometimes difficult to read for the average person, but it is firmly based on the rules and style of kaisho, the most basic form of Japanese calligraphy. If you shorten the wrong stroke, or leave out the incorrect line, the characters cannot be read or understood. This, translated into waza, means ineffective and incorrect technique. When your waza or shodo level has reached sosho, characters or techniques will appear spontaneous, elegant, effective, and well balanced. In shodo, swordsmanship, or Aikido, this journey will take many years and afford you much frustration. However, it will also provide joy, self-realization, and an understanding of the principles of *ki* and the universe.

36. Shoki: The Demon-Slayer, after Tesshu

CHAPTER 8:
SUMI-E PAINTING

*S*umi-e, also called *suibokuga*, was initially developed during the Tang Dynasty (618 -907) in China, and it became popular in the Song Dynasty (960 – 1279). (Sumi-e literally translates to "charcoal painting," while suibokuga is rendered as "water-charcoal-painting.") It was not introduced to Japan until the fourteenth century. From its onset in Japan, Sumi-e has been connected to Zen. Many people think this art epitomizes Zen principles. It is a simple art form. Traditionally, black sumi ink alone is used, so the only colors on the rice paper background are white, black, and shades of gray. The images drawn are also simple. No extraneous figures or objects are added besides the central one. In other words, only the essential elements remain. The emptiness, or void, of the artwork is as important as what is represented in ink.

Painting is a creative process, but when approached in the correct manner, it becomes a way to discover the self. As previously mentioned, Aikido has been called moving Zen and moving meditation. Sumi-e, along with Shodo, is also moving Zen. Important concepts like zanshin, fudoshin, and *isshin* are all maintained in the creation of a piece. An unknown Chinese calligrapher once said, "If the mind is correct, the brush will be correct." Before beginning, the mind must be calmly collected, completely engaged in the task at hand. Adding a few drops of water to the ink stone, it is rubbed back and forth until the proper thickness is obtained. Then, after rolling back one's sleeves, the brush touches the paper. The painter's spirit is displayed with each stroke. The final image reveals profundity. Concepts like isshin can be developed through sumi-e or other art forms, so such practices can be as beneficial to martial artists as practicing physical techniques in dojo or engaging in seated meditation. Isshin translates as "one mind," or "one heart." It is the concept of completely throwing yourself into an action. It is *hogejaku*, casting aside anything else that might be on one's mind, so that steadfast concentration can be maintained. The artist becomes one with the art. The ink flowing off the hairs of the brush contains the very energy of the creator, and thus, it becomes akin to blood – the life-sustaining liquid that contains a human being's ki.

Zen practitioners, especially those in the Rinzai sect, use art to improve their mental control. One art form that first emerged from within this sect is now known all over the world as a Zen garden. The first and most famous of these gardens is at Ryoanji (Temple of the Peaceful Dragon), in Kyoto. The property originally belonged to the Fujiwara Clan. A warlord, Hosokawa Katsumoto, acquired the property and built the temple in 1450. After, it was destroyed during the Onin War, and his son Hosokawa Matsumoto later rebuilt it in 1488. The temple houses the "Seven Imperial Tombs" of the Hosokawa Emperors, but it is most famous for the garden.

There is some controversy over who built it. Some think Katsumoto built it in the fifteenth century, but others believe his son constructed it. Still others claim that a painter and gardener named Soami (d. 1525) built it. Even more stories about the garden's creation have been passed around. The truth is, no one knows for sure who built the garden. The reasons behind its creation are also unknown. It is 248 square meters, and it is simple. The only materials used in its construction were sand, rocks, and moss. A small clay wall surrounds it on three sides, and two large wooden temple doors open on the other side, from which it is supposed to be viewed. From this vantage point, monks and temple visitors can sit anywhere they would like along the length of the garden and see almost the entire thing at the same time.

37. The famous Zen Garden at Ryoanji

However, this garden has a strange attribute: Fifteen stones of various sizes were used in its construction, but no matter where one sits to view the garden, only fourteen are visible. Perhaps the idea is to meditate until one can perceive all fifteen stones. Certainly, this type of awareness is a goal of Rinzai Zen meditation. It is also important in the martial arts. Musashi Miyamoto wrote: "Understand what cannot be seen by the eye."[35] One famous example of this awareness has been passed down, and it involves the swordsman Yagyu Munenori (1571 – 1646), headmaster of Yagyu Shinkage-ryu and friend of the famous Zen monk Takuan Soho:

Yagyu was in his garden admiring cherry blossoms. His page was behind him. Suddenly, Yagyu turned around with an angry look on his face, and he scanned the garden and surrounding walls. Then, he looked puzzled. He left the garden and remained in his quarters for the rest of the day. Eventually, his page knocked on his door and asked him if something was wrong. Yagyu explained, "When I was looking at the flowers, I got the sudden sensation I was in danger, that someone was going to attack me. I spent the better part of my life studying the martial arts and the mindset needed to become a proficient warrior. If I have imagined such a thing, it is inexcusable. I will have to train even harder."

His page then confessed, "Master, while you were watching the flowers, you did not seem to be paying attention, and I had a terrible thought. I considered how someone as insignificant as myself could still strike down a famous sword teacher if he was not paying attention. I am sorry that my thought disturbed you."

Yagyu understood why he had sensed danger in the garden, and he thanked the page for his confession. O-Sensei, the founder of Aikido, also demonstrated this ability. Once he was traveling with one of his close students, Shioda Gozo. While they were on a train, O-Sensei closed his eyes. Shioda Sensei, believing that he was napping, decided to strike him with his paper fan. Just as he began to strike, the founder opened his eyes widely, saying, "My guardian deity tells me you were thinking of hitting me. You would never do such a thing, would you?"[36] This degree of awareness is difficult to attain, and it requires a great deal of training. The combination of both martial and Zen practice is beneficial. Rinzai Zen, in particular, highlights the importance of action with complete concentration. This principle, called *samu*, is in calligraphy and the Zen art of painting: Sumi-e.

Samu is working with complete focus. To perform the brushstrokes of Sumi-e properly, the mind and brush must harmonize, just like swordsmanship, where the mind and sword must also be one. It has been said that swordsmanship and painting are the same. By looking at the bold strokes of master calligraphers, one can discern the depth of the artists' spirit and their abilities with a blade. For this reason, many well-known martial artists turned to Zen and the arts that it influenced. One of the more famous was Musashi Miyamoto, known as one of the greatest swordsmen in Japanese history.

He supposedly killed more than fifty men in duels, but it is unknown if this is true. It is also unknown if he possessed superior sword techniques or if he was simply rougher and overpowering. What is certain is his serious skill with a brush, as he left behind numerous pieces. If skill with the sword truly is revealed in that of the brush, we can surmise that he was a great swordsman. One interesting story involves many futile attempts to paint a portrait of Bodhidharma before finding success:

His lord ordered him to complete a portrait of Daruma in his presence. Musashi brought his inkstone, brush and sheets of paper, and he knelt down on the tatami and got to work. He finished the first one, but judged it inferior, so he tried again, with the same result. No matter how many times he started over, he could not finish it successfully. Musashi apologized to the lord for his failure and retired to bed. For someone who had never been defeated with a sword, failure with a brush was disturbing. He could not sleep and just lay there all night. Suddenly, a solution presented itself. Musashi jumped out of bed, lit a lamp, and finished the portrait right then and there. It was a masterpiece.

One of his disciples heard the noise and rushed in to see what the commotion was. Musashi turned to him and explained why he had failed earlier that day: when he held the brush, he held it as a painter and tried to paint. But he was not a painter. He was a swordsman. When he picked up the brush in the middle of the night to finish what he was unable to finish earlier, he held it not as a painter, but as a swordsman. Thus, the paintbrush had become his sword. Each stroke was actually a sword strike. The brush, which applied ink

38. Self-portrait of Musashi Miyamoto

to the page, sometimes thin and other times thick, maintained a rhythm, just as he would maintain a rhythm in combat using his sword. He explained this in his last text: *The Way of Walking Alone*, in which he wrote, "Never depart from the Way of the Martial Arts."[37] This document contains 21 maxims that he deemed important:[38]

1. *Do not turn your back on the various Ways of this world.*

2. *Do not scheme for physical pleasure.*

3. *Do not intend to rely on anything.*

4. *Consider yourself lightly; consider the world deeply.*

5. *Do not ever think in acquisitive terms.*

6. *Do not regret things about your own personal life.*

7. *Do not envy another's good or evil.*

8. *Do not lament parting on any road whatsoever.*

9. *Do not complain or feel bitterly about yourself or others.*

10. *Have no heart for approaching the path of love.*

11. *Do not have preferences.*

12. *Do not harbor hopes for your own personal home.*

13. *Do not have a liking for delicious food for yourself.*

14. *Do not carry antiques handed down from generation to generation.*

15. *Do not fast so that it affects you physically.*

16. *While military equipment is another matter, do not be fond of material things.*

17. *While on the Way, do not begrudge death.*

18. *Do not be intent on possessing valuables or fief in old age.*

19. *Respect the gods and Buddhas, but do not rely on them.*

20. *Though you give up your life, you do not give up your honor.*

21. *Never depart from the Way of martial arts.*

I do not agree with everything Musashi said. He was from a different era. However, the last line is significant, and it describes the mentality that any serious Budo practitioner must have. In another of his texts, the *Book of Five*

Rings, Musashi suggested that serious students explore various arts. He wrote, "Touch upon all of the arts," and he admonished those on the path to never stop forging themselves. "Forge yourself in the Way," he stated.[39] Musashi, like other great martial artists of the past, compared human beings to swords. Without polishing, their true brilliance will never be seen.

When I was with the Japanese Sword Society in Los Angeles, a man came to me with his treasure: a serviceable blade of decent quality in dire need of maintenance. I explained that traditionally forged Japanese swords require regular care and the pitting and rust on his blade would only worsen with time. To prevent it from becoming ruined, the blade needed professional polishing. I also told him it would cost (at that time) about sixty dollars per inch. When he said he was too poor to afford even one inch, I gave him this advice:

"At least you can try to keep it from getting worse," I said. "Take some oil and *uchiko* (powdered limestone), and clean it with 100 strokes on each side. Give it a final cleaning and oiling before returning it to the scabbard. Do this every day."

He nodded, and I did not see him again for several years. When I did see him again, he presented his sword to me.

"You had it polished?" I asked.

"No," he said. "I cleaned it. One hundred strokes each side, every day, for the last three years."

Intrigued, I drew the blade. Its gleaming surface was free of rust and pits: it looked professionally polished. This is why I tell my students to keep at it. Keep training. Keep polishing. Though you might be in rough shape to start with, it is amazing what can be accomplished with patience and persistence.

In my own training, I follow three paths that are joined as one: Shodo, Aikido, and Sumi-e. Musashi was only successful with the brush when he used it like a sword. These seemingly distinct paths are the same. Samu, working with complete focus, allows the artist's spirit to seep into the artwork itself. Throughout the years, I have sold many pieces of Japanese calligraphy, and I have sold a lot of Sumi-e. Like all Zennists, I am fond of drawing Bodhidharma. A bearded old monk, I suppose the portraits resemble me a bit. Once, someone who bought one of these portraits from me asked why Bodhidharma looked so mean. I replied, "As an artist gets older, his Daruma portraits start to look grumpier." I was joking, but the truth is, a Budo practitioner's spirit is revealed in all actions. A famous calligrapher's brushstrokes, or an accomplished martial artist's techniques, reveal his or her state of mind. They reveal his or her spirit, and the more one trains, the more this spirit is polished.

In time, the ego will vanish and the true spirit will shine. Hyogo Narutomi said, "What is called winning is defeating one's allies. Defeating one's allies is defeating oneself, and defeating oneself is vigorously overcoming one's own body. It is as though one man were in the midst of ten thousand allies, but no one was following him. If one has not previously mastered his mind and body, he will not defeat the enemy."[41] Mastery of the mind and body will only come about through intense training in things like Zen, art, and martial disciplines.

One of the purposes of study and practice is to take out the nails, kick out the wedges, and collapse the entire structure we build with our discriminating mind. Then the self perishes. Self is forgotten. What is the self that we so tenaciously hold onto? Some worry about nonattachment and have all kinds of ideas about it. That concern, in and of itself, is attachment. Nonattachment is not about not caring, not loving, or not doing. It is just nonattachment, not holding on, not attempting to control or manipulate. Not sticking, body and mind having fallen away is not zombie-land. Forgetting the self is not a dead person walking. It is being alive and functioning freely. This is no mind. What is your self? Is it mind? Is it body? Is it both body and mind? Is it neither body nor mind? Self is an idea. It does not really exist. We create it moment to moment. Whatever we hold onto creates a self. That is why the process of deconditioning takes so long. It is not until we are free of our attachments that we realize our true selves, and through this realization, we can begin to understand reality. The moment this occurs, the entire process is complete. The process itself is beyond time and space. Many will not engage in this pursuit, because the Path is so difficult to follow. Some will. For those of us who are following the Way, it is impossible to turn back. Forget about how fast you are, what rank you are, and who is better than who. Consider the principle of samu. Cut out distracting thoughts, and engage completely in your activities. In this way, things like calligraphy, painting, and the martial arts can help you to forge and polish yourself. These same arts will reveal your progress on the Path.

39. Self-portrait

CHAPTER 9:
MARTIAL ART TRAINING UNIFORMS

*W*hile teaching martial arts, a variety of interesting students enter the dojo. They are from different places, with unique values and customs. A man once came in with a switchblade, challenging me to defeat him. I performed a basic technique, removed the blade from him, and he later became a student. In time, his wife contacted me and thanked me, as the man had apparently stopped drinking, and he had given up his previously disruptive and violent ways. Such stories are common in martial arts dojo, as the dojo truly is a training ground, a place in which the spirit is polished and the individual is changed. Other stories do not have any kind of moral or ethical dimension, yet are funny and informative of the nature of human beings and martial arts.

We once had a dojo located within the walls of a Buddhist temple. We were short on space, so we used an area behind the altar as a changing room. First, the women changed, and then the men changed before stepping onto the mat. One evening I was late, and when I arrived, Takahashi Sensei was already teaching. Thinking that no one was in the dressing room – at least no women – I stepped right in. I was shocked to find a woman in there changing. She was naked.

"Sorry," I said.

Strangely, she replied, "No problem. Come right in."

I did not know quite what to make of this, so I stepped inside and started to change. She put her gi top on with nothing underneath and stepped out onto the mat. I knew right then that it was going to be an interesting class. The other students on the mat could not concentrate, because she exposed herself during every technique. Whether she was pinning someone or being pinned, taking ukemi or throwing someone, her breasts were visible. We had to talk to her afterward, to ask her to put some clothes on so that others could train. It turned out that she was a member of a local nudist colony. Not just that, but she had won a contest: she was Miss Nudist America. I did not even know they had contests for being naked. Anyway, she fell in love with Aikido and asked Takahashi Sensei to perform a demonstration at the nudist camp. He agreed, and they started making plans for the date and time of this demonstration. I was going to be his uke and I did not like the sound of this.

I approached him and said, "Sensei, you know that we're going to have to be naked during this demo, right?"

He said, "Yeah, I don't care. Aikido is still Aikido, even when naked."

For the next couple of days, I was worried about doing a naked Aikido demonstration in front of a bunch of other naked spectators, some of whom enter naked contests. I didn't like this idea at all! Eventually, I told Takahashi Sensei that I did not want to do it. If we were doing a demonstration, I wanted to wear a gi. He acquiesced, and we canceled the performance. The funny thing is, what we normally wear in the Japanese martial arts is nothing more than underwear.

The common (Japanese) martial arts uniform used throughout the world today is similar to historical Japanese underwear. The thinner gi-top used in karate and other martial arts was for summer, while the thicker one, used in Judo, Aikido, and other related arts, was for winter. A kimono was worn over the top of these. On top of the kimono was a *haori*, or overcoat. A *hakama* was worn around the legs, lifting up the kimono. Samurai on battlefields would tie them around their legs tightly so they would not interfere with their movement. Hakama were originally developed for early Japanese warriors on horseback. They were made of leather, and their function was to protect the riders' legs. In feudal Japan, however, leather was expensive, so hakama started to be made from heavy cloth. In time, it became less common for samurai to fight on horseback. They fought while standing instead, yet continued to wear hakama, as it had become a part of their culture and a symbol of their status.

Different types of hakama existed. The hakama commonly seen in martial arts today was called *joba hakama*, (which translates to "horseback riding trousers"). It is identifiable because it has two distinct legs. Another type of historical hakama did not have legs; it was a true skirt. Finally, there was an extremely long hakama (twelve to fifteen feet long) that was used for visitors who spoke to nobles, like the shogun or the emperor. The visitor donned this hakama upon arrival, when preparing to have an audience with his lord. Others helped the visiting samurai into this, and then folded it repeatedly as the samurai sat in seiza. This long hakama made movement difficult, so it would be unlikely that someone wearing it would ever think to initiate an attack. (It is possible that some of the seated sword kata in which practitioners do not rise to their feet to defend themselves originated with this hakama in mind. The seated techniques in Daito-ryu and the adopted forms used in Aikido might also be indirectly associated with this long hakama used in the palace.)

In modern martial arts, many people think that hakama are associated with rank, and in some arts and organizations, this is true. However, historically the hakama had nothing to do with status or rank. It was just a piece of clothing. Okumura wrote:

> In postwar Japan, many things were hard to get, including cloth. Because of the shortages, we trained without hakama. We tried to make hakama from air raid blackout curtains, but because the curtains had been hanging in the sun for years, the knees turned to dust as soon as we started doing suwari waza. We were constantly patching these hakama. It was under those conditions that someone came up with the suggestion, "Why don't we just say that it's okay not to wear hakama until you are shodan?" This idea was put forward as a temporary policy to avoid expense. The idea behind accepting the suggestion had nothing to do with the hakama being a symbol for dan ranking.[15]

Saotome Mitsugi wrote:

> "I vividly remember the day that I forgot my hakama. I was preparing to step on the mat for practice, wearing only my dogi, when O-Sensei stopped me. 'Where is your hakama?' he demanded sternly. 'What makes you think you can receive your teacher's instruction wearing nothing but your underwear?

Have you no sense of propriety? You are obviously lacking the attitude and the etiquette necessary in one who pursues Budo training. Go sit on the side and watch class!'

"This was only the first of many scoldings I was to receive from O-Sensei. However, my ignorance on this occasion prompted O-Sensei to lecture his uchideshi after class on the meaning of the hakama. He told us that the hakama was traditional garb for kobudo students and asked if any of us knew the reason for the seven pleats in the hakama.

"They symbolize the seven virtues of Budo," O-Sensei said. "These are jin (benevolence), gi (honor or justice), rei (courtesy and etiquette), chi (wisdom, intelligence), shin (sincerity), chu (loyalty), and koh (piety). We find these qualities in the distinguished samurai of the past. The hakama prompts us to reflect on the nature of true bushido. Wearing it symbolizes traditions that have been passed down to us from generation to generation. Aikido is born of the bushido spirit of Japan, and in our practice we must strive to polish the seven traditional virtues."

Currently, most Aikido dojo do not follow O-Sensei's strict policy about wearing the hakama. Its meaning has degenerated from a symbol of traditional virtue to that of a status symbol for yudansha. I have traveled to many dojo in many nations. In many of the places where only the yudansha wear hakama, the yudansha have lost their humility. They think of the hakama as a prize for display, as the visible symbol of their superiority. This type of attitude makes the ceremony of bowing to O-Sensei, with which we begin and end each class, a mockery of his memory and his art.[16]

There are two distinct interpretations of the symbolic meaning of hakama pleats. In the first, the five front pleats supposedly represent *gotoku*, the five virtues of Confucianism: *chu* (loyalty), *ko* (justice), *jin* (benevolence), *gi* (honor), and *rei* (respect, etiquette or courtesy).

Although some would say there are two pleats in the back of the hakama, only one is actually visible when looked at directly. In this first interpretation of the hakama pleats' symbolic meaning, only one is considered to exist on the back. This is indicative of an all-encompassing virtue: that of becoming a fully awakened, complete human being. Gotoku, however, is not just these five virtues.

40. Gotoku, the iron stand used in traditional Japanese homes

The Japanese term also refers to a household instrument found in traditional Japanese homes. It was the name for the iron stand that supported a kettle or other cooking pot. Traditional Japanese homes had a hearth in the central room's floor called *irori*. This was used for cooking and served the dual purpose of heating the entire house. Above the fire was a hook upon which a kettle could be hung. The kettle could also be placed on a trivet, called gotoku. This word came to serve both purposes, containing both meanings, indicating that the five virtues are something central to the home and central to a proper life. They are just as important as heat and sustenance, both provided by means of irori and gotoku.

An alternate interpretation of the hakama's pleats holds that there are not six, but seven. The one on the back, which cannot be seen, is considered.

These seven are supposed to be the seven Budo virtues, the same virtues that O-Sensei explained to his students when Saotome Mitsugi had forgotten his hakama. They are *chu* (loyalty), *jin* (benevolence), *rei* (courtesy or etiquette), *shin* (sincerity), *ko* (piety), *gi* (honor or justice), and *chi* (wisdom).

O-Sensei said that wearing a hakama is symbolic of the transference of knowledge from one generation to the next. It is a tradition that continues so the art's origins are not forgotten. The hakama, used in many traditional Japanese martial arts has never traditionally been symbolic of rank. Yet today, some schools use hakama to differentiate between yudansha and yukyusha. Only those who have attained the rank of shodan or higher wear them. Other schools ask every student to wear them. Whatever each organization or school chooses to do is fine, but it is important to remember the historical origin of this clothing, and to recognize that it is not indicative of skill. Watch how people move, not what they are wearing, and you will understand if practitioners are skilled or not.

I have had some new students in the past who might have thought that certain people (in seminars) really knew what they were talking about just because they were wearing black belts and hakama. However, the clothes do not indicate knowledge or skills. Outside the dojo, donning certain clothing could get you in big trouble. If you impersonate a police officer or wear a firefighter's or military officer's uniform you could be arrested. This is not the case in the martial arts. People can purchase a gi and hakama, and regardless of skill, experience, qualifications, lineage, or a basic understanding of the art, they can claim to be instructors. They can probably even coax a number of new students who do not know any better into their respective dojo. If they add a fancy title to their names, like shihan, hanshi, sensei, etc., they might fool even more people. It is important not to fall into this trap. Whether you are a beginner or an advanced student, try not to be attached to uniforms, ranks, and titles. Instead, focus on skill. Watch how people move, not just on the mat, but in day-to-day life. You will know what their capabilities are. In your own training, do not aim to get a black belt. Aim instead to increase your skills, with no thought about ranks or special clothing. This is the key to steady improvement and the development of true skill.

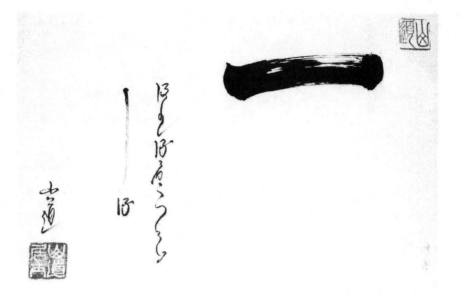

41. First, the seeker of the Way must know himself.

CHAPTER 10:
TOHEI KOICHI AND THE STUDY OF KI

I met many influential people while training at Takahashi Sensei's dojo in California, including Don Angier, who was teaching Yanagi-ryu Aikijujutsu in San Fernando Valley. This is the family martial art of the Yoshida Family of Kyushu, Japan. He is the *soke* (inheritor) of this art, having inherited it through direct succession from Yoshida Kenji, whose father was Yoshida Kotaru. Kotaru was a student and friend of Takeda Sokaku, O-Sensei's teacher. In fact, he is the man who introduced Ueshiba Sensei and Takeda Sensei in Hokkaido. While I was training in California, the Aikido Federation had just begun. We were trying to get as many dojo and instructors as possible to sign up. That is how I met Angier Sensei. We trained together a lot. I went to his dojo frequently, and he came to ours.

42. Don Angier, soke of Yanagi-ryu, and me in Tokyo.

I also met Tanahashi Kazuaki, Nishioka Hayward, Stan Pranin, and Furuya Kensho at our dojo or at Takahashi Sensei's house. In addition, I met Willis Hawley during this period. Willis was a good friend and mentor. He had a great collection of Japanese swords, Asian art, and tons of books. My wife Hana and I would spend countless hours at his home, learning everything we could about Japanese swords and Asian art forms. It was due to his influence that I joined and later became the president of the *Nanka Token Kai*. He taught me *kanji*, the Sino-Japanese characters, and seal carving. I helped him put together a two-volume book on Japanese swords called *Japanese Swordsmiths*. One of them has a Sumi-e painting of a samurai on the back cover that I penned. Along with the other Sword Society members, we organized a Japanese sword exhibition at the Barnsdall Museum. This was a major event. A Masamune sword was sent from Japan for display at the exhibition, and the Japanese Ambassador was present.

Masamune Goro (ca. 1264-1343) is considered one of the finest Japanese swordsmiths in history, if not the best. He made blades of all lengths in the *Soshu* style, and today they are worth millions of dollars. It is thought that he worked in Sagami Province during the end of the Kamakura Period (1288-1328). An interesting legend is told about this swordsmith, although it is of dubious historical accuracy. His student Muramasa challenged Masamune, and they had a contest to see who could forge a finer blade. They both went to their forges, purified themselves, and then began creating their blades. They worked without rest. Eventually, they both completed their work, and got together to inspect each other's swords.

They decided to test the cutting capabilities of the blades. Muramasa plunged his blade into a river's flowing water, and it cut everything that passed, leaves, sticks, fish, and other creatures. No life was spared. Masamune then dipped his sword into the river, and the opposite occurred. Sticks, leaves, and fish moved right around the blade without being cut. All lives were spared. Masamune withdrew his sword, shook the water from it, and then sheathed it. Muramasa thought that he had won, that his blade was superior, until a monk who had witnessed the event came over to explain what actually occurred:

The first of the swords was by all accounts a fine sword, however it is a blood-thirsty, evil blade, as it does not discriminate as

Although this particular tale might not be true, Masamune blades are considered to be lucky, truly "life-giving swords," while Muramasa blades are supposed to be unlucky "death-dealing swords." Both of these blades are worth a fortune, and it was therefore incredible that we were able to display a Masamune at the sword exhibition.

I trained with and talked to many well-known martial artists and authorities on East Asian art and history during this period. One of the most influential was Tohei Koichi, who did more to establish Aikido, as it is known today, than anyone else. He was the chief instructor at Hombu Dojo in Tokyo for many years, and his contributions should be constantly recognized and praised. He was, without doubt, the most important figure in Aikido's early history, (insofar as its development and diffusion is concerned).

43. Tohei Koichi instructing outside the dojo in Hawaii. I am sitting directly behind Tohei Sensei. Next to me is Bob Frager. Furthest right is Suzuki Shinichi.

When I first got involved in Aikido, Tohei Sensei had written the only worthwhile book on the subject, and it was influential in my Aikido studies. It was called *Aikido and the Arts of Self-Defense*. He was the chief instructor at the Aikido Hombu Dojo, and the founder later awarded him tenth-dan in 1969. It seems that a book was influential in his pursuit of martial arts as well. He was a frail child, and he began studying Judo at Keio University to grow stronger. He became sick with pleurisy, though, and had to take some time off. His sister bought him a book called *My Teacher*, which was written by Ogura Tetsuju, one of Tesshu Yamaoka's students. Tesshu is often referred to as Japan's last great swordsman. He had incredible power, and he trained not just in swordsmanship and the martial arts but also in Zen Buddhism. The book mentioned a type of ascetic training that was done in a dojo called Ichikukai. Tohei was interested, so he went to this dojo, and he learned that they still followed the hard-core training practices that Tesshu taught.

He wished to train at the dojo, and he decided to do whatever they told him to do, even if it killed him. When he arrived, they would not let him in the door, stating that the training would be too intense for him. It involved shouting in a loud voice and being struck repeatedly on the back. They told him it was unlikely that he could handle such abuse. However, he was resolved to become stronger at any cost, even if it meant his death. So he continued to show up, asking for permission to join. Eventually, the headmaster of the dojo, Hino Tesso agreed to let him practice zazen, seated meditation. Tohei Sensei meditated all night long. None of the other students did this, but the chief instructor agreed to sit with him for as long as he would like. In this way, he received direct instruction in some of the techniques that made Tesshu Yamaoka so powerful.

In time, the meditative practices made him stronger, as they were indeed a body-changing method. He was later x-rayed at a doctor's office, and they were surprised to see that there was no sign whatsoever of him ever having pleurisy. Once his body was strong enough, his instructor allowed him to participate in the other, more extreme practices, which they grouped under the heading of *misogi*. Misogi is often referred to as ritual purification, and is carried out in many religions worldwide, only under different names. In Japanese religious traditions, misogi is performed upon entering Shinto shrines, when visitors pour water on their hands and mouth as a basic gesture of purification. Ascetics in northern Japan often doused themselves with cold water daily. The term was eventually used to describe a variety of ascetic practices other than purification through water; it came to label all sorts of asceticism in both martial arts and religious traditions.

Tohei Sensei continued to train at this dojo, but he also returned to Judo. He had been away from the art for almost two years, and while he was gone, people who were once as skilled as him had advanced, and they now threw him easily. In an effort to catch up, he made it a part of his daily regimen to kick the support beams of his home 2,000 times. His family did not like this, as the walls started to come down. They made them go out into the yard instead. Eventually, this training paid off, and he was as comfortable using his feet and legs as he was using his hands. When he returned to the dojo, he was able to throw everyone.

Years later, Mori Shohei Sensei told him about a powerful martial art instructor named Ueshiba Sensei, and suggested that he train with him. He gave him a letter of introduction, and Tohei showed up at the dojo. An uchideshi named Matsumoto greeted him at the door. Tohei Sensei asked him about the art that was taught there, and Matsumoto demonstrated kote-mawashi on his left wrist. Although it was painful, Tohei threw a punch at him with his right hand, and Matsumoto released him. This initial display of Aikido did not impress Tohei Sensei. However, at that moment, when he was thinking about leaving and never coming back, Ueshiba Sensei showed up. As a demonstration, he began throwing some of the senior students around the dojo. Tohei's first impression was that it looked fake. Then, O-Sensei invited him to attack, and he was thrown so effortlessly that he could not determine how it was done. He ceased training at the Judo dojo, and began studying Aikido full-time.

He was amazed at O-Sensei's power, and he could not figure out how some of the techniques were done. The other students at the dojo were able to throw him easily, including high school students. This was a mystery at the time, but he continued training. He also continued to train at the Ichikukai. Instead of sleeping, he would often stay there overnight practicing zazen and misogi the entire time. Although exhausted, he would then head straight to the Aikido dojo to train. He came to realize that after spending the entire night engaged in such ascetic practices, people at the Aikido dojo were no longer able to throw him. It was then that he realized the power of complete relaxation and ki energy.

Ki, means "energy" but it is extremely difficult to translate because of the many nuances that the term suggests, including, "nature," "intention," "disposition," "feeling," "attention," and more. In the Japanese language, numerous expressions make use of the term. For example:

> *Ki ni suru:* literally, "to do ki," means "to care about something or someone."

> *Ki o momu:* literally, to "knead one's ki," means, "to worry."

> *Ki o shizumeru:* literally, "to quiet one's ki," means "to collect or compose oneself."

> *Ki o tsukeru:* literally, "to attach one's ki," is properly translated as "to pay attention" or "to notice."

> *Ki ga omoi*: literally "heavy ki," means "to feel depressed."

> *Ki ga kawaru*: literally, "ki changes," means "to change one's mind."

> *Ki ni naru*: literally "to become ki," means "to weigh on one's mind," or "to be troubling."

> *Ki ga chiisai*: literally "small ki," means "to be timid or shy."

As is immediately evident by looking at this term's use in the Japanese language, it is not easily defined. When using the word in the context of the martial arts, it generally refers to intent, and when one extends his or her ki, it is the act of extending intent. When people begin training in martial arts, they learn stances and try to perfect physical techniques. Initially, they might try to power through resisting opponents, using muscular strength. After years of training, practitioners who reflect upon their progress will eventually come to realize that muscular strength is always weak. There is something more to the martial arts. It is at this point that they begin to train in ki development. Tohei Sensei just realized this fact a bit sooner than most people did. He explained:

I was not able to relax immediately; my ability to do so, and to use ki instead of strength, simply evolved naturally the more I trained. My Aikido continued to progress as I continued with my misogi and zazen. After six months or so, I was even sent to teach at places like the Military Police Academy in Nakano and the private school (juku) of Shumei Okawa. No one except Sensei could throw me. It took me only six months to achieve that degree of ability, so I think taking five or ten years is too slow. Even now, most people are trying as hard as they can to learn techniques, but I was learning about ki from the beginning.[18]

During World War II, he had to stop training, as he was called into action. He had close calls with death on battlefields, but his training in misogi and zazen had given him peace of mind, and he began to think that the universe had more planned for him – that he would not die in battle. He explained:

Once I made that decision, I suddenly became much more at ease, and after that, no matter how intense the fighting became, the bullets did not hit me. Gradually, I became bolder – perhaps even arrogant – and I told my men that if they followed me, bullets would not hit them. They all believed this, and at the time, mine was the only company to come back with all 80 men unscathed. From that experience, I realized that the universe must have a mind of some sort.[19]

When he returned from the war, he began training in Aikido again. O-Sensei was able to throw him, but others could not. He began to wonder why. He wondered what type of training O-Sensei had undertaken to make him so powerful. This obsessed him, and he studied ki and methods of developing ki power with even more fervor. He trained with Tempu Nakamura Sensei (1876–1969), who developed a mind-body training method called Shin Shin Toitsu Do. It contained elements of Indian yoga, some martial art practices, and other methods for ki development. Nakamura Sensei explained to him that the mind must lead the body. Most people in the martial arts try to control the opponent's body, but Tohei Sensei believed that the founder did not do this. Instead, he first control the opponent's mind, which in turn, affected the body. In this way, Tohei Koichi's study with Tempu Nakamura provided some means of understanding what O-Sensei was actually doing.

After much training and some hands-on experience, he determined that the most important lesson O-Sensei had given him was how to relax. O-Sensei was always completely relaxed as he performed techniques, and this relaxed condition made techniques effective. In 1953, Tohei introduced the art to the United States where he faced strong Judo practitioners in Hawaii. He learned first-hand that being relaxed was much smarter than tensing up:

> When you're firmly pinned or controlled, the parts of your body that are pinned directly simply can't move. All you can do is start a movement from those parts that you can move, and the only way to do that successfully is to relax. Even if the opponent has you with all his strength, you can still send him flying if you are relaxed when you do the throw. This was something I experienced first-hand during that trip to Hawaii, and when I returned to Japan and had another look at Ueshiba Sensei, I realized that he did indeed apply his techniques from a very relaxed state.[20]

After Tohei Sensei had introduced Aikido to Hawaii in 1953, he continued to come to the States for extended periods in which he taught the art. He often came to California and stayed for weeks at a time. He always stayed at Takahashi Sensei's house, so I had the good fortune of spending some serious time with him. He loved German food and beer, and a great restaurant served authentic food nearby. We often went there after class. I learned a lot from him both on and off the mat. He taught me how to relax and extend ki, which made my Aikido techniques much more powerful.

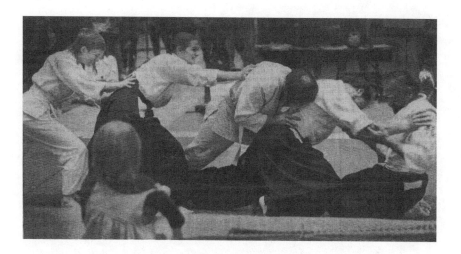

44. Demonstrating the power of ki in Montana (c. 1983). Here, four students push on me. (photographer unknown)

Most Aikido practitioners are familiar with pictures of the founder seemingly rooted to the ground. While in a seated or standing position, he had numerous students push on his head, shoulders, or other parts of his body, to demonstrate that he was immovable. Tohei Sensei also performed this feat on numerous occasions, and he taught me how to do it. I still use some of those techniques to demonstrate the power of ki. This ability does not come about by some sort of magical or religious training. It is an actual technique that must be learned and practiced, although it might not be described in the same terms used for physical techniques. It is a ki technique. When becoming immovable, I make myself as heavy as possible, and then extend ki in all directions. The same technique is found in some other internal martial arts, and the Chinese even have a specific term used to refer to this training. They call it pulling-silk. Aikido practitioners are not really practicing the art that the founder did if they are not learning and practicing these techniques. Certainly, the term ki is within the Sino-Japanese characters for Aikido. Without ki, there can be no Aikido. I am grateful to Tohei Sensei for teaching me such things.

Tohei Sensei was personable, and everyone seemed to like him. He taught many of the most famous Aikido instructors that instruct today, including Tada, Arikawa, Yamada, Chiba, Okumura, and Yamaguchi.

Stan Pranin described Tohei Sensei during this period:

Indulge me for a short while as we board together a time machine to the golden years of Aikido's infancy in the U.S.A. in the mid-1960s. We see a different landscape when compared to the art of today. The name of Koichi Tohei is on everyone's lips. He is now in his vigorous 40s, handsome, charming, and physically gifted. He is a fluent speaker of English, the author of best-selling books on the art. He is supremely confident, a wonderful teacher. He is the chief instructor of the world headquarters dojo, the Mecca of Aikido, and he is the "ambassador of ki." Yes, Koichi Tohei is the man every devotee wants to see in the flesh, the one whose techniques are to be emulated, [and] the one who inspires. His interpretation of techniques represents "the" standard. His views on the principles of Aikido and the "mysterious" concept of ki are unending topics of conversation. He is the motive power driving the spread of the art. Koichi Tohei IS Aikido![21]

I was fortunate to receive instruction from him, Takahashi Sensei, and all of the other individuals with whom I interacted up until 1967. It was at this point that I made the decision to go to Japan and train with the founder himself. In 1966, Takahashi Sensei came to my house, suggesting that I go to Japan while O-Sensei was still alive. At first, I did not want to go. Like all human beings, I was resistant to change, but after his continued prodding, I agreed that it was important for me to meet him. At first, I did not know how I would afford such a trip, but I was determined to do anything. My wife Hana was supportive, and we decided to sell our house. Armed with a letter of introduction from Takahashi Sensei, I headed to Tokyo, Japan.

45. Tenchi, Heaven and Earth

CHAPTER 11:
MEETING O-SENSEI

46. One of the few color photographs of O-Sensei. Picture taken (c. 1967).

*I*n 1967, O-Sensei did not have a scheduled class at Hombu Dojo. He showed up when he wanted and taught what he wished. I was lucky that when I showed up at the dojo for the morning class, he happened to be there. After the class had ended, Bob Frager brought me to his office and introduced me. O-Sensei was kind. He smiled, welcomed me, and then proceeded to talk for about a half hour about things I could not understand. I was not alone; it turns out that few people could understand him, because his talks were seemingly a nonsensical combination of esoteric Shinto ideas, Omoto-kyo ideology, and practical martial art methods. He even quoted from the Chinese Classics frequently. Many of the senior students did not even try to understand what he was talking about; that is how difficult it was to comprehend.

Tohei Sensei said that O-Sensei often said nonsensical things, and he sometimes found it difficult to express himself without falling back on Omoto-kyo spiritual ideas. While his other teacher, Nakamura Tempu was quite humble when Tohei Sensei approached and asked questions, O-Sensei seemed quite the opposite. He explained:

The only thing of true value [O-Sensei] taught was how to relax. But that is all right, because a person only really needs to have one thing of value to teach for you to make them your teacher. The only thing I learned from Tempu Nakamura, for example, was that "the mind leads the body." On all other matters, he used to ask me questions! He was very modest and humble in that respect. When I said that I did not know the answer, he would then say, "Well, let us study it together then." Ueshiba Sensei, on the other hand, would say things like, "There is nothing that I do not understand; the things I say even scholars and saints are incapable of understanding, and even I, though I am saying them, do not understand..." It is impossible to understand this kind of talk.[22]

There are countless examples of senior students talking about how they could not understand the things that O-Sensei mentioned. One of the more interesting involves O-Sensei's trip to Hawaii in 1961. They were opening the Honolulu Aiki Dojo, and Ueshiba came from Japan to bless the location. He was there for the opening ceremony. Tohei Koichi and Tamura Nobuyoshi accompanied him. A reporter asked O-Sensei some questions, with Tamura functioning as a translator, and they were unable to translate his speech. No one knew what he was saying. Eventually, Tohei Sensei filled in the gaps and added some clear wording, and the article was completed and then published, but it was definitely not what O-Sensei had said. Other senior students expressed the same comprehension difficulties. Koroiwa Yoshio said, "I hated [his lectures]. He would talk about the Kojiki and things, but my legs would fall asleep and I couldn't understand anything. It just made me cry."[23]

47. O-Sensei was deeply religious, and his talks were exceedingly difficult to comprehend.

Nishio Shoji said, "No one listened to what O-Sensei was saying... Because he spoke like a kami-sama (god) they thought that nothing he said could be understood, and didn't even try to pay attention when they were listening."[24] It was not that people did not care, but his speeches were just that difficult to understand.

Languages contain unique words. Lithuanian, for example, has terms for multiple shades of gray, and the Japanese language has numerous words for a fish called the gray mullet, differentiated by the age and size of the fish. Other Japanese terms have no direct equivalent in other languages, terms like *wabi* and *sabi*. The former means something like "refined elegance" or "unpolished beauty." The latter is similar, but conveys a sense of loneliness. Such words cannot be easily understood by speakers of different languages and from diverse cultures. When trying to understand such concepts, listeners might be confused, or they might believe that they understand even though they are mistaken. Thinking of these examples might help to understand the problems that students had when trying to understand O-Sensei's speeches. He seemed to have his own terminology, which does not directly translate into other known languages. This made comprehension difficult. Upon meeting him for the first time, I too had the same difficulty. O-Sensei was a complicated individual, and he created the martial art Aikido based upon two paths: Daito-ryu Aikijujutsu was the marital side of the equation, while Omoto-kyo was the spiritual side.

According to legend, Daito-ryu was handed down by a legendary warrior named Shinra Saburo Minamoto no Yoshimitsu (1045-1127). He lived in a mansion called Daito (Great Eastern Palace) in Omi province, modern Shiga prefecture, which is from where the art's name stems. Yoshimitsu supposedly studied the Chinese Classics and other books about military strategy, and he learned about the human body and how to control joints by dissecting corpses. Aiki is said to have originated in the art of *tegoi* and been passed down as a secret martial principle of the Minamoto clan. However, this history cannot be verified, and it is therefore much more likely that the art was developed by Ueshiba Sensei's teacher, Takeda Sokaku.

Takeda Sensei was an interesting person. Highly distrustful of others, he always carried weapons. He killed numerous people, and he almost killed his own son in an episode that is informative when trying to determine the type of person that Takeda was:

One day Takeda Sokaku was sleeping, and Soke (Tokimune) wanted to put a cover on him to keep him warm. Sokaku, always being in a state of awareness, even when sleeping, grabbed his dagger and went to stab Soke in the heart just as Soke was about to put the cover over Sokaku. Soke was barely quick enough to move to the side, got off the line, and the dagger that was going for his heart stabbed him in the shoulder. Afterwards, Takeda Sokaku scolded his son severely saying, "What kind of fool are you?! You should never carelessly come up on someone by surprise! It is your own fault that you were stabbed. If you would have been aware I would not have cut you!" That's the kind of man Takeda Sokaku was."[25]

Daito-ryu does not show up in Japanese historical records before Takeda Sokaku. It is likely that he learned some jujutsu techniques that were handed down in the Takeda clan, although such techniques were perhaps not grouped under a specific name. To these he added jujutsu techniques that he learned from others. Another important concept was added to Daito-ryu Aikijujutsu, and without it, Aikido today would not exist. He added aiki to the techniques. It is unknown exactly where he learned this specific art, although it has been rumored that Tanomo Saigo, also known as Hoshina Chikanori, taught him such skills. Aiki is a specific technique that can be used within other techniques. In other words, it is applied throughout the application of jujutsu. Daito-ryu has three different levels of waza. Jujutsu techniques are throws, pins, and strikes that utilize the opponent's strength, his momentum or natural weak points, to control an attack. Aikijujutsu techniques make use of aiki, which dissolves the attacker's power along with the regular jujutsu techniques. The final category is aiki no jutsu, which is just aiki without any jujutsu techniques. Seeing these techniques performed by modern Daito-ryu teachers, small movements are used to disrupt the opponent's balance and control him.

48. Takeda Sokaku, O-Sensei's teacher

To get an idea of how this structure of techniques would be used in Aikido, consider the following: *ikkyo*, as it is done in typical dojo, is the jujutsu version of the technique. (One blends with the opponent's movement and applies the technique to unbalance him.) If aiki is added to the application, it is the aikijujutsu version, and if the particular aiki technique used in its application is retained, but the joint manipulation is removed, the aiki no jutsu variation appears. Regarding aiki itself, Sagawa Yukiyoshi explained, "By taking the stance that aiki is a technique, that something is there, you can slowly begin to understand it. Nothing will come out of the thinking that aiki is the flow of ki or the art of go no sen – reacting by provoking the opponent to attack first."[26]

He also wrote the following to explain aiki further:

> *The fact that I can do what I do even though I am more than 80 years old is proof that aiki is a technique. Because it is a technique, you can get better and better at it even as you get older. Takeda Sensei used to talk a lot about the technique of aiki – in other words, what he was saying was that aiki is a technique. To call it "ki" or the "flow of ki" – it's nothing like that. If all you needed was ki, that would be nice, but it doesn't work like that.*[27]

Aiki was the major skill and high-level teaching that O-Sensei learned from Takeda Sokaku, and he used this as a base in his own martial art. Aiki is so difficult to do that few have this skill, but O-Sensei had it, as did his teacher Takeda. Among the hundreds of jujutsu techniques used in Daito-ryu, O-Sensei only adopted a handful, which became the techniques used in modern Aikido. At first, O-Sensei taught Daito-ryu Aikijujutsu. It was not until he met Deguchi Onisaburo, the head of the Omoto-kyo religion, that Aikido as it is known today was developed. This religion came to dominate O-Sensei's life, and its influence on him cannot be overstated.

The founder of Omoto-kyo was an illiterate woman, Deguchi Nao (1836-1918), who claimed to have become possessed by a little-known Shinto deity named Ushitora no Konjin. This spirit told her to pick up a brush, and by the time she died, she had penned about 200,000 pages of text, all of which she was never able to read herself. This became the holy text of the Omoto faith, and her writings were known as *ofudesaki*, which literally translates as "from the tip of the brush." She attracted numerous followers, and a religion began to take shape around her prolific prose. It was not until Deguchi Onisaburo (1871-1948) got involved that the religion became famous.

49. Deguchi Onisaburo, O-Sensei's spiritual teacher

Onisaburo's real name was Kisaburo. He married Nao's fifth daughter and adopted her name, thus making himself a part of this expanding religion. He was an eccentric man, often exposing himself in public or modeling costumes that he designed. He was an artist, and he left behind thousands of calligraphic works. He also made pottery, and he believed that artwork was important in the development of the spirit. Deguchi often disguised himself as Buddhist and Shinto deities, both male and female, and claimed to be in the incarnation of Maitreya, the Buddha of the Future, who would establish a new heavenly kingdom on Earth.

Deguchi Onisaburo and Aikido's founder Ueshiba Morihei traveled to Mongolia in an attempt to begin a heavenly kingdom there. Deguchi claimed he was the Khan of Mongolia. He also referred to himself as Sakyamuni and the Dalai Lama. Not surprisingly, they ran into some opposition, and O-Sensei had to kill bandits with his sword. Another time, they were shot at while traveling along a mountainous road. O-Sensei later said that he could sense when the bullets were coming and was therefore not concerned with being shot. Although this feeling might be nothing more than overconfidence, it is interesting that both O-Sensei and Tohei Sensei both experienced this sense of calmness while under attack.

50. Statue of Maitreya (Aomori, Japan)

The authorities later arrested the group in Mongolia, and they were sent to be executed. They were certain that they would die. Deguchi said a final prayer, and he, O-Sensei, and the other members of the group lined up before a firing squad. At the last moment, someone arrived from the Japanese consulate who secured their release. Perhaps due to some of these experiences with life and death, O-Sensei began to change his outlook, and the art now known as Aikido began to take shape.

Omoto philosophy stresses four principles: purity of mind and body, optimism, progressivism, and unification. These ideas carried over into Aikido. Regarding purity of mind and body, O-Sensei said, "Always try to be in communion with heaven and earth; then the world will appear in its true light. Self-conceit will vanish, and you can blend with any attack." In accord with the principle of optimism, he said, "Protectors of this world and guardians of the Ways of Gods and Buddhas, the techniques of peace enable us to meet any challenge." Progressivism is revealed in his statements too, for example: "Even though our path is completely different from the warrior arts of the past, it is not necessary to abandon totally the old ways. Absorb venerable traditions into this new art by clothing them with fresh garments, and build on the classic styles to create better forms."

Unification, like the other three principles, is an important concept in the creation of Aikido. Deguchi Onisaburo said:

> *The teachings of Omoto are not those of a single sect. We do not believe, as do many established religions, that in the words of our founder we have the one and only religious truth. At Omoto, we do not bind up and destroy peoples' living souls by encircling them with the steel nets and bars of doctrines and scriptures and rituals and catechisms. As a result, Christians, Buddhists, and believers of other faiths from all over the world come to Omoto, and we all work together to cultivate our spirituality and to discover religious principles in harmony with our times.[28]*

Ueshiba Morihei likewise said (about Aikido), *"The Art of Peace is the religion that is not a religion; it perfects and completes all other religions."*

O-Sensei combined the martial and the spiritual paths, and he created Aikido, which he perceived as something much greater than a normal martial art. Perhaps it was his experiences facing life and death in Mongolia, or his later experiences, seeing people he knew and loved die during World War II that did it, but somehow, he came to believe that Aikido could unite people. Techniques originally designed to maim or kill were modified so that ukemi became possible. Now, these same techniques can be used as exercise, and students can throw each other quickly and smoothly without risking serious injury.

O-Sensei was a remarkable man and a Budo genius, and I was overwhelmed to sit in his office in Tokyo, Japan, knowing that I would be learning from him directly. I wanted to learn all that I could, and preserve as much of his knowledge as possible. (At the time, the only English-language book about Aikido was Tohei Koichi's *Aikido and the Arts of Self-Defense*.) I felt it was important to transcribe as many lectures as possible. Some of these lectures appear in this book in subsequent chapters. When I was learning from him, I kept a diary, in which I recorded some of his statements, my interpretations of them, and some artwork that I felt best represented the ideas. Some of these items are also included in this book, and I hope that they benefit martial artists of all disciplines, not just Aikido. As O-Sensei intimated, Aikido is not a martial art. It joins all martial arts together.

51. Suchness

CHAPTER 12:
A TYPICAL CLASS TAUGHT BY O-SENSEI

52. O-Sensei in his office

*M*ost of the classes at the Hombu Dojo were not taught by O-Sensei, but by one of the senior students. Although Tohei Sensei was still the official chief instructor there, Ueshiba Kisshomaru Sensei and Okumura Shigenobu Sensei taught many of the classes. Shimizu Kenji Sensei was one of the senior students. He was especially polite and helpful, and I am grateful to him for his assistance. O-Sensei showed up about once or twice weekly to teach. The senior students led the classes. They bowed in, did some warm-up exercises, and then demonstrated a technique, which we would practice. O-Sensei generally showed up after this. Since everyone was already training, he did not spend much time on warm-ups. However, he did lead us in some stretching. Usually, we stretched for about five minutes, and then he always did *funakogi undo*, the so-called "boat-rowing exercise" that all Aikido students practice.

This exercise, which is a variation of one found in some Chinese martial arts, helps to develop a strong foundation. It also teaches students how to move from their centers and use the hips properly. First, stand in a natural posture in which your feet are about shoulder width apart. This natural posture, called *shizentai*, is an important base from which to execute proper techniques. Before explaining the specific steps in the funakogi undo exercise, it is important for students to understand how to stand properly in Aikido and other martial arts.

In Aikido, the basic *hanmi* is called *sankaku-tai*. It is based upon the goal of building a unified body. Underlying this important principle are the following concepts:

1. **dynamic stability**

2. **minimal muscular tension**

3. **non-obstruction of the normal functioning of internal organs**

4. **the ideal that proper form must be considered in all things**

Shizentai literally means "natural body," but it refers to maintaining the correct skeletal posture. If the spine is not in the correct position or the body is not centered, you will be unstable. Here are some rules that will help you to maintain the proper stance:

1. **Both legs should be perpendicular to the ground, while keeping the inner thighs parallel.**

2. **Strongly pull back the pubic bone.**

3. **Extend the spine by stretching it upward.**

4. **Extend the breastbone outward.**

5. **Pull back the chin.**

6. **The hips and shoulders should be level in relation to the floor.**

7. **The nose and naval should be perfectly aligned.**

All of these things should be done naturally, subconsciously, and without extremes. Refrain from action contrary to nature. O-Sensei said that correct posture is indicative of the mind's proper state. Certainly, learning how to stand correctly is a prerequisite to being able to perform an exercise like funakogi undo properly. Once you are able to stand correctly, you can begin this exercise:

Inhale and step forward with your left foot. Move both hands forward like you were rowing a boat. Then, with the kiai "e," move your hips backward and follow them with your hands and arms. Next, with the kiai "ho," return to your original position. This should be performed twenty times. Then switch your stance, and with the right foot forward, repeat the same exercise using the kiai "e" on the forward movement, and "sa" on the return movement.

While performing this exercise, it is important to remain centered. Your body weight should never be on the left or right side, as this would make you unstable. O-Sensei always talked about the importance of being centered and stable. It is especially important to practice such body movements during basic exercises. Besides remaining centered during funakogi undo, make sure that you concentrate on your lower abdomen, the *tanden*, and extend your ki in all directions. Move in a relaxed manner. With proper posture and strong intent, think about rowing to an external ideal world, thus improving your own mental state, but also increasing the desire to improve society and life in general.

Typically, in O-Sensei's classes, after we did this exercise, we would all sit down. We did not sit in straight rows like many dojo do today. Rather, we sat in a circle around him. Sometimes, he demonstrated a technique, always using Shimizu Kenji as uke, after which we practiced. Other times, he would talk for an hour or more about Aikido or spiritual and religious concepts that many people struggled to understand. Some of the younger students found it difficult to sit for such long periods, and the pain in their legs captivated their minds; they were unable to pay attention to the message conveyed. When he started talking about esoteric concepts, using terms like *kami*, we assumed that he was referring to Omoto-kyo ideas. He also talked about the triangle, circle, and square. He once explained these concepts in the following way:

The body should be triangular, the mind circular. The triangle represents the generation of energy and is the most stable physical posture. The circle symbolizes serenity and perfection, the source of unlimited techniques. The square stands for solidity, the basis of applied control.

Using this definition alone, the concept seems simple to understand, but there are many levels of meaning in the concept behind these shapes.

53. The triangle, circle, and square

CHAPTER 13:
THE TRIANGLE, CIRCLE AND SQUARE

*T*he triangle, circle, and square describe metaphysical concepts in various traditions. They are not unique to Omoto-kyo and Shinto. They are in many other faiths, including Buddhism. The underlying concepts that the symbols represent are multifaceted, so they are difficult to understand. Aikido too should be difficult to understand. If it looks like Aikido and you understand it right away, it is not Aikido. Real Aikido requires a lot of study. Likewise, understanding the complete significance of these three seemingly simply shapes might require decades of learning. If you get overwhelmed reading the following explanations, just fall back to O-Sensei's simplified version: "The body should be triangular, the mind circular. The triangle represents the generation of energy and is the most stable physical posture. The circle symbolizes serenity and perfection, the source of unlimited techniques. The square stands for solidity, the basis of applied control." However, what follows is the metaphysical explanation for the shapes' importance:

The square represents earth, matter, human beings, solidity, love, and compassion. In Vajrayana and Mahayana Buddhism, it relates to the number four: the four periods, four seasons, and the time of the Tathagata, which is the period of correct teaching, the semblance of the teaching, and the decadence of the teaching. It also relates to the four abodes, the goodness of heart, joy, *samadhi* of the immaterial realm, and samadhi of the infinite. The term samadhi is interpreted differently in various Buddhist sects. In a general sense, it is mental concentration and development. There are four stages of this development:

1. First, abiding pleasantly in this existence, which is achieved through concentrating on the four dhyanas. (These are types of meditation, which result in various stages of awakening.)

2. Second, knowledge and an understanding of the divine eye, which is attained through concentration on light.

3. Third, mindfulness and clear understanding, which develops from the mindfulness of feelings and thoughts, in other words, perceiving such mental activities as an outside observer.

4. Finally, the destruction of the taints, which is achieved through mindfulness of the five aggregates. These components make up a human being: form, sensation, perception, mental impulses, and consciousness. In the Zen tradition, Samadhi is considered the same as Prajna, the mental capabilities that enable one to distinguish between right and wrong and to live without erring. One who has attained this state is considered to have awakened, and he or she is called a Buddha.

The square also relates to and symbolizes the four attachments: desire, false views, false morals, and ideas stemming from the concept of self. O-Sensei said, "Joy is the greatest treasure." This joy is expressed metaphysically in the concept of the square. It appears in Aikido under the guise of *shiho-nage*, or four-direction throw. This is related to *shiho-hai*, which is performed during some Shinto religious ceremonies. It is a symbolic action in which the performer demonstrates gratitude in all four directions.

The triangle is the mystical trikona. Trikona is a Sanskrit word that means "triangle." The symbol is used in various kinds of meditative exercises, just as some use mandalas as an aid. A triangle positioned upward indicates man, phallus, and yang ("yo" in Japanese). It also symbolizes of the Vedic god Agni, Linga (a representation of Shiva), and Purusha, the first form of the Supreme Lord Narayana, who pervades all things in the universe. He is equivalent to Mahavairocana (in Sanskrit), or Dainichi Nyorai (in Japanese): the Cosmic Buddha. If the triangle is pointed downward, it represents water, yin ("in" in Japanese), the womb, and nature, specifically mother nature. When two triangles are joined, one pointed downward, the other upward, it indicates creation and the unification of opposites. It is the interaction between yin and yang, fire and water, which gives rise to all things.

The triangle is associated with the symbolic body position of Padmasambhava. It represents the three treasures: the Buddha, the Dharma, and the Sangha. It also symbolizes yoni, the source of all things in tantra and mantra. The Buddha spoke about the symbol of the self-using three points, which were arranged in the form of a triangle. It is the Tathagata. It also represents fire, which is yang ("yo" in Japanese). It is the mudra of crossing the sea of life and death by means of concentration. This concentration can help one to arrive in a state of Nirvana. It can help one to achieve enlightenment. This is what O-Sensei called *iku-musubi*, tying up the life force.

The triangle can also be associated with the three sacred treasures of Japan's indigenous faith, Shinto: the mirror, sword, and jewel. It might also be connected to the concept of *tenchijin*, heaven, earth, and man, which is an important Aikido concept. The technique *tenchinage*, or heaven and earth throw, is quite possibly a physical representation of the same concept. When O-Sensei performed this technique, his physical posture was the *abhaya mudra*, in which one hand points toward the heavens, while the other is down, pointing at the Earth. The triangle is also represented in the Sino-Japanese character for mountain, which actually represents three mountains. The middle one is higher than the other two.

54. Three Merging Mountain Paths

My Buddhist name, Sando, is written with the character for mountain and the character for path or way. In the Japanese written language, mountain has the inherent meaning of three because it originally represented three (sacred) mountains. If the first character for mountain is replaced with the kanji for the number three, it is pronounced the same way. I had always considered that this reference to three had to do with my study of three paths, which I see as leading to the same place, the same summit: Shodo (calligraphy), Sumi-e (ink-painting), and Budo (the martial arts), all of which manifest Zen. I jotted some thoughts about this in my notebook, and I have included that page herein (fig. 54). When thinking about the nature of the triangle, however, I began to think that there was more to it, that there was a deeper meaning that I had not yet unlocked. Certainly, this is what the lifetime pursuit of Budo does. The more one learns, the more one realizes how little he or she knows. There is always something more to study and pursue, and there is no end. This never-ending cycle is perfectly illustrated by a circular shape, as there is no real beginning and no real end. They blend seamlessly.

The circle connects to the Shinto sacred mirror. It is a void, for it reflects all factors of the phenomenal world, but it deprives them of substance. The phenomenal world is thus illusory. All substance is illusory, as everything in existence is nothing more than the subjective idea that individuals have about it. The mirror makes it known that no transitory factor in existence has any more self-reality than a reflection, which is presented in the mirror. It thus represents the notion of understanding what material illusion is: ideas are contrasted with phenomena. When this symbol is carried by Avalokiteshvara, the Bodhisattva of Compassion, it represents Akshobya Buddha (or Ashuku Nyorai), the immovable one. This Buddha is the embodiment of the mirror, which reflects everything and reveals what is real and what is illusory. Contained within him, and within the sacred mirror, are all images throughout space and time, yet he is not moved by them; he remains unaffected by such sights. In the martial arts, *suigetsu* (moon on water) is an important concept, and it is the same. Yagyu Munenori (1571 - 1646) wrote:

The mind is like the moon on the water.

Form is like the reflection in a mirror.

This verse suggests that the mentality proper for the martial arts is that of the moon's abiding in the water. It is also the reflection of your body abiding in the mirror. Man's mind moves to an object like the moon moves to the water. How spontaneously this happens![31]

The moon reflected upon water is the highest mental state of a warrior, as he sees opponents move and attack, yet remained true to himself; he is un-flustered by such attacks. Feeling no fear, he can act with complete freedom. Therefore, he emerges victorious.

O-Sensei said that the unification of the three shapes and concepts results in one integrated form. When this form is infused with ki, stillness in motion is achieved. When the triangle, circle, and square are represented together, the triangle is typically on top. In the middle is the circle, and the base of the shape is the square. This same pattern is seen in Buddhist graveyards: me-morial stones' shapes follow the same pattern. The triangle can be associated with ki, the energy that is driven by intent. The circle can be related to *kokoro*, which has the alternate pronunciation *shin*. This can be translated as heart or spirit. The square can represent human beings. The following diagrams, from the notebooks I kept in Japan, might help to clarify the complex relationship between the phenomenological and spiritual concepts represented by these three fundamental shapes.

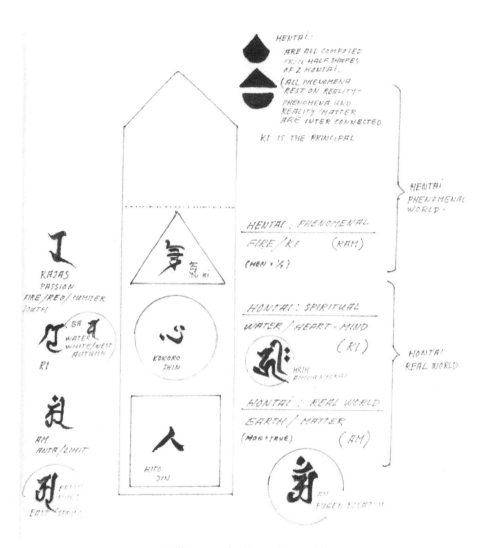

HENTAI :
ARE ALL COMPOSED
FROM HALF SHAPES
OF 2 HONTAI.

(ALL PHENOMENA
REST ON REALITY-
PHENOMENA AND
REALITY/MATTER
ARE INTER CONNECTED

KI IS THE PRINCIPAL

HENTAI
PHENOMENAL
WORLD.

HENTAI : PHENOMENAL
FIRE / KI   (RAM)
(MEN = ½)

HONTAI : SPIRITUAL
WATER / HEART - MIND
                (RI)
HRIM
AMIDA NYORAI

HONTAI : REAL WORLD
EARTH / MATTER
(MON = TRUE)   (AM)

HONTAI
REAL WORLD

RAJAS
PASSION
FIRE / RED / SUMMER
SOUTH

(BA
WATER
WHITE / WEST
AUTUMN)
RI

AM
ANTA / LIMIT

EARTH
FIRE ?
EAST / SPRING

气 ki

心
KOKORO
SHIN

人
HITO
JIN

AM
FUGEN BOSATSU

55. Notes on the three shapes (1)

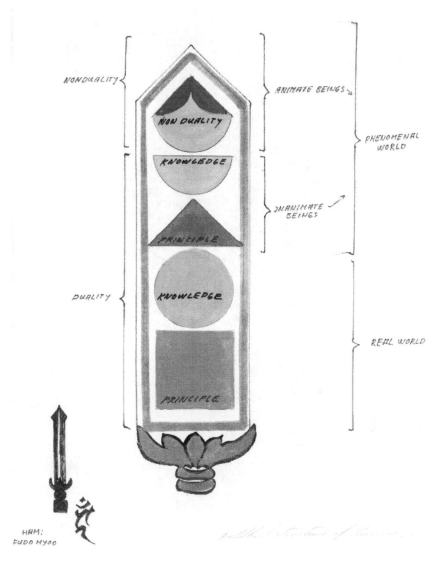

NONDUALITY

ANIMATE BEINGS

PHENOMENAL WORLD

NON DUALITY

KNOWLEDGE

INANIMATE BEINGS

PRINCIPLE

DUALITY

KNOWLEDGE

REAL WORLD

PRINCIPLE

HAM:
FUDO MYOO

56. Notes on the three shapes (2)

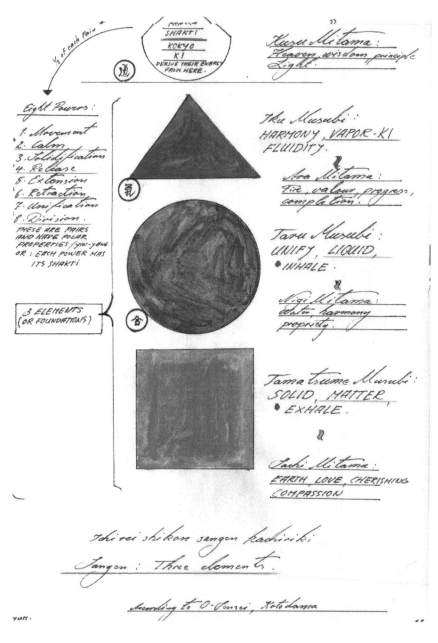

½ of each Pain →

SHAKTI
KOKYO
KI
DERIVE THEIR ENERGY
FROM HERE.

Kuzu Mitama:
Heaven, wisdom, principle
Light.

Eight Powers:
1. Movement
2. Calm
3. Solidification
4. Release
5. Extension
6. Retraction
7. Unification
8. Division

THESE ARE PAIRS
AND HAVE POLAR
PROPERTIES (yin-yang
OR : EACH POWER HAS
ITS SHAKTI

Iku Musubi:
HARMONY, VAPOR-KI
FLUIDITY.

Ara Mitama:
Fire, valour, progress,
completion.

Taru Musubi:
UNIFY, LIQUID,
• INHALE.

Nigi Mitama:
Water, harmony
propriety.

3 ELEMENTS
(OR FOUNDATIONS)

Tamatsume Musubi:
SOLID, MATTER,
• EXHALE.

Sachi Mitama:
EARTH, LOVE, CHERISHING
COMPASSION

Ichi rei shikon sangen kachiriki.
Sangen : Three elements.

According to O-Sensei, Kotodama.

YUM.

**57. Notes on the three shapes (3). For more information on this topic, please see
John Steven's book The Secrets of Aikido.**

O-Sensei talked about the significance of the shapes, and he often talked about the importance of center and centering. These two concepts are inherently associated with the circle.

O-Sensei said:

> To fall in with the movements of the circle is the technique and essence of Aikido. The movements of technique act upon the body and the buildup of these effects is the tamashii [spiritual essence] of the circle. This circle is in the all-void, and that which is born out of the center of this void is the kokoro [heart]. The all-void is free and self-existing. When a center arises in this space, ki is created. The life-producing and ki-generating power in the immeasurable and infinite universe that arises out of the void's center is the spirit. This spirit is indestructible and has produced everything that exists. When one has acquired the circle in the whole being of one's body, it creates the elemental foundation of all techniques. This productivity is without limit, ever changing and adoptable. This is takemusu. The circle becomes the means that fulfills all needs most profusely. The circle gives birth to forms that protect and bring to completion all that exists and all that live in the entire universe. This is ki-musubi and iku-musubi [tying up ki and tying up life]. In this world, even the karmic action of cause and effect is in harmony with the circle and round movement. The spirit of Aikido is circular. To understand Aikido and bring together the physical and the spiritual in such a way where both aspects live and prosper is to create the circle of the soul. All the ki in the universe is appeased and well controlled by the circle of tamashii. Without this, the entire cultivation of the physical body comes to nothing. The emptiness or void of the essence of the circle comes to be the harmony in the universe. This is the root of the spirit of Aikido and it is the secret principle revealed when this tamashii is mastered and understood by the body. Embraced within this circle are the movements of mutual destiny and all things are understood as if held in the palm of

your hand. When you cultivate tamashii, it is also for the benefit of others. When all things are solved freely, then you understand the secret principle of the circle. This is the act of giving birth to techniques by moving freely, adopting and not being attached to useless methods, by thrusting to the very center of the void.

I spent a great deal of time thinking about such concepts, and I even wrote a poem that helped me to make some sense of it all. The following is the English translation of it: The sharp-edged sword, unsheathed, cuts through the void. Within the raging fire, a cool wind blows.

58. The Circle, the Essence of Aikido

CHAPTER 14:
CENTERING

*T*he idea of the center, and maintaining one center, is directly related to the shape of the circle. In Aikido, we hear a lot about center and centering, but most students are not taught how to center or what the center means beyond the obvious, which is balance. When O-Sensei talked about center, he was not speaking just about physical shapes and how you move the body. He was referring to a spiritual center: the center of all things. This can also be thought of as the center of all centers. All things, physical and spiritual, emotions and energies, are grouped around this center. Picture yourself surrounded by a group of other people. Although you are in the center, all of those other people also have centers. The center to which both Aikido and Zen refers preexists all others.

It is important to understand the other centers in your own mind and body. If you do not understand their function, you will never find the true center, which originated before all others. It is your true self, and an understanding of this center is equivalent to the Buddhist idea of enlightenment. Wrong use of the minor centers within the body can yield intellectual, emotional, or physical dis-ease. Your life will be out of balance if they are not controlled. From a physical standpoint alone, your body will be out of balance if you do not maintain your center. Concentrating on one over another, the physical or the spiritual, is ineffective. In your training, you must learn to perceive the spiritual and physical centers. You must strive to understand and control them all.

It is tempting to classify all centers and their functions according to whether they are interfering with the work of another center, or working with energy intended for another function. However, it is difficult to put these into simple categories, so do not try to categorize them. Just observe them. Observing these centers helps you use your energy more efficiently, and it will help you to resist transient, habitual identifications. In general, every center wants to acquire the most volatile energy that happens to be present in you at any moment. Each center wants to enhance itself. It grabs what it can when its power rises in you.

The instinctive center is the strongest and most persistent function. It is aware of energetic changes in your body. It allows itself to exploit its connection to false personality, channeling energy and the power that goes with it to the centers that it chooses. It allows the instinctive mind to keep you continuously dazed by your own activity, unable to change the basic ways in which energy is ingested, processed, and distributed within your body. The result of this process is that little energy appropriate to each other center is available to it at the time it is needed. This results in a disjointed and unconnected body. To have physical power in your movements, it is important that the entire body move in unison. When one thing moves, everything moves.

When this bodily connection is not maintained, and the ki flow does not sustain each of the energy centers equally, other centers end up working with too much or too little energy. All functions have an order of dominance based upon their relative levels of development and maturation. Those that are more active take energy and control from the weaker, less developed functions. They therefore end up functioning at a lower capacity. For this reason, the centers' work is frequently destructive, chaotic, and disharmonious. It is important in spiritual disciplines and in physical disciplines like the martial arts to become aware of this complex interaction between centers. True mastery will only occur if all of the centers are brought into control, and the mind and body work together in unison. The body must be unified, and this unification is achieved with the mind. O-Sensei said, "When attacked, unify the upper, middle, and lower parts of your body."

Rather than trying to understand the complex interrelationships between all of these centers, and the connection between mental and physical centers, simply attempt to observe them. Become aware of them. This awareness will help you to use your energy more efficiently. From a physical standpoint, you will become more difficult to unbalance and throw. From a mental standpoint, you will be steady and unmoving. This is the Zen concept of no-mind.

To attain this mental state, one must train both the mind and the body. It will not happen on its own. If you are mindless, just going through the physical motions in the dojo, you are not training your mind. Your energy is not sustained in all the right centers. You must completely devote yourself – mind and body – so ki energy can flow appropriately. In this way, true power can be developed. When the body moves, the mind must be completely absorbed in that movement. Form follows intent, so intent must drive the motion. In time, this focus and devotion will increase your ki power, and it will lead to mushin. Swordmaster Yagyu Munenori said, "See first with the mind, then with the eyes, only then with the body." The mind must lead.

Do not misunderstand this and become concerned with how the opponent is reacting to your technique. You must quit all desires, including the desire to restrain an opponent or to emerge victorious in a bout. If the mind is properly controlled it becomes selfless, devoid of desires. When this occurs, it will be constantly at peace. No one, neither friend nor foe, could disturb it. When the mind does not move, true skill develops, and techniques flow forth spontaneously. This is what the founder called Takemusu Aiki.

59. Takemusu Aiki

CHAPTER 15:
TAKEMUSU AIKI

*T*akemusu Aiki, as perceived by O-Sensei, is the highest level of the martial arts. It is not confined within the art called Aikido, nor is it a straightforward concept. It is multidimensional, and like everything done in the martial arts, it contains many layers of meaning. To understand it properly, it is best to consider the overall practice of the martial arts. When students first begin, they attempt to learn the proper postures. They need to learn how to stand correctly. Then, having understood how to maintain correct body posture, they then learn the physical techniques of attack and defense. After years of this kind of training, they are ready to add additional layers.

Students learn how to extend energy. They learn this from a stationary posture, and it is demonstrated in Aikido and some Chinese arts by teachers who ask many of their students to push on them while either in a seated or standing position. As onlookers will attest, they are immovable. O-Sensei demonstrated this frequently. Tohei Sensei did too. I have even demonstrated it for skeptical audiences. This is a basic ki training exercise. Once students learn this simple technique, they need to learn to take it a step further. There is always another step to take. They need to learn how to remain heavy, rooted to the ground, while extending energy in all directions in motion. They need to remain immovable while moving and performing techniques. After students progress in this facet of training, another emerges.

At the beginning, stances and movements were awkward, as the students' bodies had not yet been changed through training. In time, they perfect the outward form, but they still have to think about it. In time, the correct body movements for the specific art studied become natural. The student no longer has to think of them, as the correct movements have become natural. At this point, the true stance is no stance. Watch videos or look at pictures of O-Sensei. His stance, throughout all of his techniques, is nothing more than a natural stance, *shizentai*. He never assumed what others would call a martial stance, because all of his stances were martially effective. No matter how he stood, he never provided an opening.

60. O-Sensei demonstrating a technique. (Shimizu Sensei is uke.)

One of his uchideshi, Yonekawa Shigemi, explained the importance of not providing an opening, as taught to him by O-Sensei:

One day when I had answered a phone call from outside, O-Sensei came up behind me and tapped me on the shoulder. He said, "When you are talking on the phone, you are completely off-guard. That is simply careless. Keep in mind that even if you think it is just a telephone call, you should clearly exhibit a posture of readiness for attack at all times." He would scold me in this way. Sometime later, someone said to me, "Whenever you come through a door, you need to be completely alert in all directions."[29]

The same progression does not just happen with stances. It also occurs with techniques. Eventually, the (correct) movements become so engrained that it is difficult to do anything but the techniques that have been repeatedly trained in the dojo. Once this occurs, onlookers who do not know much about martial arts will think that the defender is a master. However, he or she might just be a performer, a rehearsed example of correct stances and the proper form of techniques. For many people, their training stops at this point. Even if they continue training for years after this point, they do not progress, as they are not practicing in the correct manner. At this point, students must learn to move beyond form and techniques. The founder said, "You have to forget about technique. The further you progress along the path, the fewer teachings there are. The true path is no path."

Aikido is not a martial art of forms. Aikido is the study of spiritual energy, a formless power. Techniques, therefore, should be based upon formless energy, not outward forms. This is takemusu (and tai no henka). Some people practice only form and become attached to what they see and feel. I am not referring to maintaining good stances, balance and center. Although you need to start with the outward forms, you must not become preoccupied with them. Once you begin to understand and sense the formless, you realize that the formless forms give rise to harmony and beauty. Forms are only an introductory system for learning foundations. If you only train forms, and not the spiritual or internal aspects of the art, you will only improve up to a certain point. You will never become a master. You will only look at others through form, and you will possibly make comparisons, trying to determine whether they are better or worse than you are. You will cling to outward symbols, which ultimately do not matter. In any field of study, outward forms are only to point the way toward the development of the spirit. Even when one walks into a temple and sees a large statue of Buddha, adherents do not believe that the Buddha in the statue is a living entity. Instead, the statue's outward form helps students to train the spirit. It is just a form, which is an expedient. To improve continually in any discipline, not just the martial arts, you must move beyond set form.

A great example of this principle is found in the tea ceremony: One of the most acclaimed masters of all time, Sen no Rikyu, taught both of his sons everything he knew. Another cannot give true mastery, though. It is attained only after years of discipline and effort. One son built a wonderful teahouse and garden, using all of the dimensions and particular instructions that his father had imparted. It was visibly perfect. He invited his father, the wise old master, to look at his creation. Sen no Rikyu arrived smiling, but upon seeing the complete adherence to the teachings that he had imparted, his smile turned to a frown. The son realized that something was amiss. He thought about it, and then hurried over to a cherry tree in the garden and shook the branches, thus allowing the blossoms to cover the ground. At this gesture, his father smiled, for he recognized his son as a true master of the art.

When forms have been forgotten, and techniques arise spontaneously based upon the situation at hand, takemusu aiki is demonstrated. Aikido is neither for dominance nor for competition. It is for spiritual growth. O-Sensei said the following, which I recorded in my notebook:

People who think of Aikido simply as a martial art do not improve beyond a certain point no matter how much they practice. In order to help them, shihan should always talk about the spiritual aspects of Aikido. To help students, especially above shodan, you need to make them realize that their ki will not extend unless they help beginners. A shodan training with another shodan will

not learn to extend his ki no matter how long he practices. As he
starts practicing with beginners, his ki starts extending.

As the founder suggested, it is important to think of Aikido as something more than a martial art. Think of it as a spiritual study, but also think about the inherent study of ki. If you only train with students at the same level, you know how they will move and react, so you become trapped, but if you train with students and teachers who are better than you, and others who are not as good as you, you will become prepared for anything, the orthodox and the unorthodox, and your ki will extend. This is how improvement happens.

Shinpin Fumetsu
Indestructibility of the sacred.

61. Shinpin fumetsu – The indestructibility of the sacred.

CHAPTER 16:

AI-KI-DO

*G*oi Masahisa (1916-1980) was the founder of the Byakko Shinko Kai religion. His writings became the faith's foundation, which holds that human beings are not sinful by nature. Rather, since all life forms emerged from the Divine Source, each life form has divinity within. This is similar to the Buddhist idea that all humans can become Buddhas only by discovering their own inherent Buddha natures. When O-Sensei met him, he reportedly said, "I am the universe." Goi Masahisa, referring to him, wrote:

Ueshiba Sensei, the founder of Aikido, entered into the World of Infinite Dimensions. He achieved Oneness with the Universe and, therefore, even though he is an old man, only five feet tall, when three or four strong, young men try to push him over with all their strength, they can never succeed. Ueshiba Sensei keeps smiling, then he moves just slightly and all those young men are thrown down. After that, a group of people attack with wooden swords, but they are also thrown into the air with this one simple move. Ueshiba Sensei can do such things, and the reason why he can is because he is One with the Universe. He is the Universe itself and, of course, there is nothing more immense than the Universe. He is not a physical body and freely enters into God's mind. No one can ever strike God, of course. He is in the world beyond three dimensions, beyond this merely three-dimensional world. Thus, no matter how you try to hit him, he is not there. However, you see his physical body and believe that he is there. The truth is that, even though you see him as a physical presence, he is not there because he has merged into the Universe and become One with it. Therefore, when you go to strike him, you will be struck yourself by your own intention of striking. The law of cause and effect of your thoughts work

---

> *in this manner: If you want to hit someone you will be hit. If*
> *you want to defeat someone, you will be defeated. Even the*
> *strongest champion boxer will lose his match in the end. He will*
> *surely lose his championship. Thus, if you want to strike a blow*
> *against someone, that thought will revolve around the Universe*
> *and come back to you. When you attack Ueshiba Sensei, who is*
> *the Universe itself, you will be thrown by the power of your own*
> *mind. Ueshiba Sensei needs but a single movement in order to*
> *throw you. He is a man who has achieved such a state of being.*[33]

When people who do not know the techniques used to perform such seemingly impossible feats try to explain what they have seen, they describe them as miraculous. Goi Sensei did not understand some of the methods used by O-Sensei and his students, such as remaining immovable when pushed, so he related it to a divine power. Obviously, it is not. An actual technique is used to transform the body, connecting it to the ground so that it cannot be moved. This technique involves ki, which animates the body.

O-Sensei's statement, in which he referred to himself as the universe, might seem strange and inexplicable, unless one actually understands the perception of ki as found in Japanese religions and martial arts, specifically Aikido. Tohei Koichi perhaps did more than anyone else (in Aikido history) to introduce this concept to outsiders. He explained the concept of ki in a manner similar to O-Sensei's explanations, and his explanation can clarify the master's statement, in which he claimed to be the universe:

> *Anything that has form must have a beginning. For example,*
> *the sun is said to be blazing now, but there must have been a*
> *beginning to the fire. There must also have been a fire before*
> *the fire started. If we trace the origin of all things, we reach a*
> *point at which nothing existed. On the other hand, nothing*
> *cannot give birth to something. Zen uses a term mu, which*
> *means nothingness, but not a complete nothingness; that is,*
> *the Zen term mu means a state in which, though nothing exists,*
> *there is still something. Mathematically speaking, the basic*

entity of mathematics is the number one. The earth is one. A pebble is one. If it is reduced to half, what remains is also one. If it is reduced by half infinitely, it does not become zero. If there is one, half of it always exists. Ki is the infinite gathering of infinitely small particles. In this way, the sun, stars, earth, plants, animals, and human mind and body, are all born of the ki of the universe. From ki, the real substance of the universal, came movement and calm, joining and breaking apart, tensing and slackening, and many mutual actions which gave the present universal its form. Ki has no beginning and no end; its absolute value neither increases nor decreases. We are one with the universal, and our lives are part of the life of the universal [ki]. Since before the beginning of the universal, and even now, its absolute value exists as a solid fact within which birth and growth and death and dissolution continue to take place. The Christian Church calls the universal essence God and its action God's providence. In other words, God exists in this world and God's providence is a never-ending process. In Ki Society, we make a distinction between the ki we use every day and the universal ki.[32]

All people have this energy source within themselves, so individual ki can be discussed. When O-Sensei and other great martial artists discussed extending energy in techniques, they were referring to the individualized ki. This smaller concept of ki constitutes human beings, which are nothing more than composites of their flesh and egos. But this energy source stemmed from the universal energy source, so all things are connected. This is the universal ki. Once human beings realize that their ki is connected to the ki of the universe, they are approaching enlightenment. This is what O-Sensei referred to when he mentioned the unity between himself and the universe. It was a statement between one religious man and another that revealed his spiritual attainment. This understanding of energy does not come to many people, and if you believe you have understood it right away, you are far off the mark. It takes years of training, and it is best to begin by understanding how to use this energy in practical martial arts applications.

The way ki works resembles how a sound resonates and causes vibrations. This is called *hibiki* (resonance) in Japanese. Without hibiki, your ki cannot reach other living beings. With hibiki, you guide the opponent into your movement. You need to remove his ki and strengthen your own. To remove his energy, you must first blend with his energy, merging with his ki. If this first step is bypassed, harmony (*wa*) cannot be attained. Joining your energy to his energy is called (*ai*), and it is the first Sino-Japanese character in the word Aikido. Ai is attained when your ki and your opponent's ki resonate together. Once this merging of energies occurs, they become one. You can then lead the opponent where you want. O-Sensei explained this in many ways. He said, "Opponents confront us all the time, but there is no real enemy there. Enter into an attack and neutralize it as you pull his power into yours." On another occasion, he explained, "Even powerful human beings have a limited sphere of power. Pull his outside the sphere and his strength will disappear." Understand that your energy and your opponent's energy are actually the same, since they both originate within the universal ki. If you can grasp this concept, in time you will learn to blend with attackers.

O-Sensei explained how to harmonize with attackers:

> You must learn ki and kokoro. Kokoro is the center, which turns in a spiral. What helps kokoro to revolve is ki. Therefore, ki and kokoro must be harmonized and become one. This allows you to become one with the opponent. Think about it.

This statement will likely confuse anyone who has a basic understanding of the Japanese language. Linguistically, kokoro, which can also be pronounced "shin," does not mean center. The term means "heart" or "mind." The famous author Soseki Natsume (1867 – 1916) wrote a book entitled *Kokoro*, which was translated into English as *The Heart of Things*. However, O-Sensei had his own type of language, and when he used this term, he (sometimes) meant "intent." In this particular quote, it is likely that kokoro refers to the *hara*, and ki means intent. The definitions he gave to terms were not always consistent.

Ki can only be controlled through intent. Some basic Aikido training exercises can help beginning students to understand how to make ki move through intent, including the so-called "unbendable arm" exercise. Practitioners place their arms, elbows down, on their partner's shoulders, and their partners clasp their hands over the elbow joint, applying pressure downward. First, the practitioners try to prevent their arms from bending with muscular force. This provides a way to compare between muscle and ki energy. Once they have tried this and failed, it is now time to do the exercise correctly, using ki. They now relax completely, keeping a slight bend in the arms. As their partners apply increasingly more downward pressure, they strive to relax even further, imagining that their arms were something like a fire hose: water is flowing through the arm and out the fingertips. They will find that they are much more powerful with this visualization and while remaining completely relaxed. This is only a basic exercise for beginners to grasp the importance of relaxation and energy development. It is up to each individual student to study and progress further.

O-Sensei provided some advice:

Ki does not flow unless you breathe, unless you use kokyu-ryoku [breath-power]. Ki is a difficult concept to master. Many people talk about ki without knowing what it is. Ki is part of kokyu. Ki is born of kokyu. Ki is everything. Your whole being becomes ki. Correct breathing is kokyu. You have to know how to use the power of kokyu to master the power of ki.

As the founder points out, there is a relationship between breathing and energy. When martial artists perform techniques on others, they must do so while exhaling. It is best to attack opponents when they are inhaling, as their ki is not extended. O-Sensei said, "There is exhaling and inhaling ki. In practice, you should learn how to use this. You cannot throw someone while inhaling. Energy gets flowing as you exhale in harmony with your waza."

He also explained how the eyes must be used: "If you are throwing this way you should not be looking the other way. You must look at where your ki is going. You must look at the future path of the ki flow!" This statement is reminiscent of Yagyu Munenori's admonition: "Seeing with the eyes come second to seeing with the mind." The mind creates the intent with which to lead ki. The eyes follow that movement. The correct use of the eyes reveals many advantages. When performing techniques, if I look where I want the opponent to go, it is easier to lead him there. Here is an example outside of the martial arts to clarify this: Suppose I walk into a crowded train station and stop in the center of the room. People would continue on their way and not give me a second look. But if I start staring at the ceiling, a few people next to me might do the same. Others would see us looking at the ceiling and want to know what we are looking at, so they too might look up. This will cause a chain reaction, just by the use of the eyes, nothing more. The same natural human tendency can be exploited in the martial arts. The eyes must follow energy. Your techniques will become stronger, and your partners will be more easily led.

The first character in the term Aikido, Ai, has to do with meeting and then redirecting the attacker's energy. Ki refers to extending your energy in all directions, thus overwhelming your opponent's energy and redirecting it. The final Sino-Japanese character, *do*, is also pronounced *michi*, meaning "path" or "way." When this character is used in the Japanese martial arts, it indicates something spiritual. It indicates that the arts are being used for a higher purpose. Aikido shows us clearly and relentlessly who we are and how we define the limits of our cage, the ego. If one can perceive the difference between one's own ki and the universal ki, one can begin to understand the unity of the two. The only true enemy is oneself. It is only by dissolving the perceived separation of the self and others that we can be truly present in the moment. When this occurs, we develop a mind that allows us to meet any situation with freedom and fearlessness. This is the mind of no abode. It is also known as mushin, no-mind. O-Sensei explained this clearly: "If you have not experienced true emptiness, you will never understand Aikido." This non-abiding mind is like a mirror, clear and unobstructed. It harmonizes with all that it encounters. This is the mind developed in the practice of zazen. When this mind becomes our everyday mind (in life), we are walking the path of harmony. This is the "do" character in Aikido.

62. Hogejaku. Throw it all away.

CHAPTER 17:
SOME JAPANESE GANGSTERS

*A*t some point in their lives, serious martial art practitioners want to test their progress. They do not want to undergo rank tests; that is not what I am talking about. They want a real one, possibly a life or death scenario. Japanese and Chinese martial artists' biographies are replete with such tests. One famous example in Japanese accounts involves a sword master testing his three sons. He placed a pillow above a doorway and devised a way to make it fall upon anyone who stepped beneath it. He invited his three sons to enter the room, one at a time. The first son came through the door, and was surprised to sense that something was falling. He jumped aside, drew his sword, and cut the pillow in two. The father put another pillow in place, and called the second son through. The same thing happened: the pillow fell. He was shocked, like the first son, but he noticed that it was a pillow and not a real threat, so he did not draw his blade. Instead, he caught it and then looked inquisitively at his father, who smiled. Again, he repeated the test for the last son. The third one sensed that something was above the door, and he reached through the doorway and removed it before stepping through. He had obtained the wisdom and insight needed to perceive what others could not. He was judged superior to his brothers, and he became the inheritor of his father's sword art.

It is unknown if tests like this actually took place. They might just be lessons passed down in the guise of an actual historical tale, but serious martial artists like to test their skills. When some of the high-ranking Japanese Aikido instructors first came to the United States, they used to have what they called "watch night." They would go out to rough areas, bars and nightclubs, and wait. Eventually, someone would try to pick on the small Japanese men, and they would be forced to defend themselves. After it was over, they would take the attacker's watch. At the end of the night, whoever had the nicest watch was deemed the winner. This might not be just, but it is common. In Japan, we also wanted to test our skills outside the dojo.

Across the street from Hombu Dojo were some restaurants and food stalls, and along the same street were some nice *izakaya*, drinking places. Beyond that, on the other side of the railroad tracks, was a known yakuza hangout, where we were told not to wander around. It was too dangerous. After class, some of the other foreign students and I would go out, get some drinks, and then walk around yakuza territory, hoping for some excitement. Occasionally, I was able to test my skills. One time, however, we ran into some trouble. We were walking along the road, and someone walking behind me was saying bad things about foreigners. I smiled, thinking that we were going to have some fun, but then I looked back and noticed three strong men. I did not think a physical engagement with them was a good idea, but I did not know how to get out of the situation.

I noticed that the man saying bad things was encouraged by his two friends. I stopped, turned around, and said to him, "Why is a good-looking man like yourself hanging around with these two losers?"

The other two instantly became riled up and started talking about beating me up, but the man who was previously mouthing off now tried to calm them down. He said, "This guy is ok. Leave him alone."

They did not let it go and their conversation quickly became an argument. That is, until the first punch was thrown. The three men began fighting each other, even though they had previously been working in unison focusing on my friend and me as potential enemies.

I did not know what I had done, if this was some martial arts principle put into practice, but I thought about the incident. I think that there is a lesson to be learned in the way this event turned out. It could have ended in so many different ways. O-Sensei said, "The Way of a Warrior is to stop trouble before it starts. It is defeating your enemies by making them realize how futile their actions are." The more I considered this, the more I came to realize that this event was an example of takemusu aiki. Many consider that takemusu aiki refers to expansive, ever-changing physical techniques alone, but the same principles can be carried out in non-physical ways. True takemusu must never stop evolving and expanding. It must even expand beyond the realm of physicality.

O-Sensei said that constant change, improvement, and evolution are the hallmarks of a great martial artist. This is takemusu. Expansion of the ideas and the system of Takemusu Aikido are limited by the nature of the ideas themselves. They are also limited by students' inertia and their inability to understand these ideas. Sagawa Yukiyoshi said, "To do aiki requires first a brain. Stupid people can never do aiki. And training. It's hard enough to get it even with training; there is no way that someone who doesn't train long and hard will ever understand aiki."[30] Students must train hard and they must go back and actively think about what they are practicing in the dojo. They must study.

Have you ever noticed how much of our practice focuses on studying? We are not members, adherents, patients, or clients. We are students. The emphasis is on learning, and to learn we must be open and ready to learn about ourselves. Zen master Dogen reminds us that study is self-empowerment. No one can study for you, and you cannot bypass it and buy the result. You have to do it for yourself. This requires discipline. It requires constant reflection, because without reflection, there can be no growth.

Takemusu Aiki should be limitless. Students who do not spend the time to understand these concepts impose the only limits. Expansion of a martial art and a martial artist is necessary. Before this expansion can be properly considered, it is important to understand what a martial artist is, as there is a lot of confusion. There is no better place to start than the actual meaning of the words: "martial" in general has to do with armed combat, military endeavors, or war, as used in terms like "martial law" or "martial state." This word stems from the Roman god of war, Mars. The term "artist" is defined as a person who performs or exhibits a specific skill or talent. In the West, martial artist is a word used to describe any individual who trains in an organized structure using specific weapons or unarmed strategies as a discipline. Fencing, boxing, wrestling, shooting, and even horsemanship are martial arts, so anyone who practices such arts can be considered a martial artist.

In Japan, old combat arts are called *bujutsu, heiho,* or *koryu.* The character "bu" in bujutsu consists of a spear clashing with a sword. Beneath these two clashing weapons is the character for *tomeru,* meaning, "to stop." In this way, the character that is often translated as "martial" is actually the opposite. It refers not to inciting violence, but rather to stopping it. Thus, the martial arts are actually arts of peace. This is not a mystical, spiritual perception of such arts, but the real interpretation based upon a pictographic, linguistic analysis.

The word "bu" is also used in the term "bushi," which generally translates to "warrior," but it should now be evident that this translation is approximate. It is not accurate. (The word "samurai" uses a different ideograph, a different Sino-Japanese character, and is not associated with the word "bushi.") Martial arts that end with the word "do," like Judo, Iaido, and Aikido, are not considered combative arts. The original arts, which contained the suffix "jutsu," were more martially oriented. There is a hazy line between the so-called modern "do" arts, and the koryu arts, which made use of names ending with "jutsu." In most cases, the techniques used are similar, if not the same. The difference between the modern arts and their predecessors is spiritual attitude. It is a different approach to training, in which a practitioner studies with an aim toward self-improvement. To study the Way is to study the self. To study the self is to forget the self. And to forget the self is to be enlightened by the ten thousand things.

Sui-getsu:
Moon and Water

63. Suigetsu. The Moon abiding on Water

CHAPTER 18:
BUDO AS A SPIRITUAL PURSUIT

64. O-Sensei and his wife Hatsu

One morning, I left my dorm and walked to the dojo's main entrance. O-Sensei was out front. I said good morning, and we were on our way inside together. The children's class had just ended, and some of the kids were exiting the building. One of them did not recognize O-Sensei, and he asked, "Aren't you too old for Aikido?"

O-Sensei was known for sudden, angry outbursts, so I stood there, speechless, waiting for what happened next. O-Sensei calmly asked, "Who is your teacher?" He asked this question because the first thing any assistant instructor should do is introduce new students to the chief instructor, or in this case, the art's founder. I slipped past him into the dojo, and I wondered what kind of a class it would be.

After changing, I stepped onto the mat, and class began as usual, with one of the senior students leading us in warm-ups and then demonstrating some techniques, which we practiced until O-Sensei appeared. We all sat down, and he followed his normal routine: stretching for a few minutes, funakogi undo, and then *furitama*, the "shaking the ball" exercise. This is an exercise that many practitioners frequently do but rarely talk about. Viewed by outsiders, it looks like students are simply shaking their clasped hands in front of their abdomens – an inexplicable movement performed for an unknown purpose. Here is how the exercise should be performed, and the reasons behind it as I interpret what I have been taught:

Stand in a natural posture, with the feet about shoulder width apart. Straighten the spine and connect to the ground. Make yourself heavy, and then extend ki in all directions. In this way, your body connections will be strengthened. Focus on the lower abdomen, the spot called the tanden, which is located about three inches lower than the navel. Direct your eyes as though they would be fixed in seated meditation: they are neither completely open nor completely closed. They are relaxed, and you are seeing yet not seeking to see. You are simply taking in what is around you without any attachment to it.

Inhale. Place your left palm on top of the right palm, clasping your hands lightly together. Shake your hands while maintaining the ki energy in all directions, so it is not just your hands moving, but everything. You will not see excessive body motion externally, but if people put their hands on you, they would feel it internally. This exercise builds the connection between the hands and the center, and it trains the hands and arms to become infused with ki. This exercise also has a spiritual component, and O-Sensei always used to highlight this aspect of it.

When performing the exercise, empty your mind. Become calm. Once you stop shaking the hands in front of the tanden, pause. Remain in this position, immovable. Feel as though you are united with heaven and earth. The spiritual purpose of this exercise is to cultivate self-awareness. O-Sensei explained this exercise using esoteric Shinto and Omoto-kyo ideas, which were difficult to follow. He used the names of gods from the Shinto sacred texts *Kojiki* and the *Nihon Shoki*: the left hand was Izanagi, and the right hand was Izanami. This is understandable.

In the native Shinto faith, all things were brought into being by the creative aspects of these two deities. Izanagi was the male or yang force, while Izanami was the female or yin power. The procreation of these two was the symbolic representation of the interaction between yin and yang, which is the source of all creation and the secret to performing aiki. O-Sensei made other statements regarding these two deities and the forces they represent, including the following: "Takemusu is the harmonization of fire and water; that interaction is the divine techniques of Izanagi and Izanami." In furitama, O-Sensei also equated the left foot to Ame no Tokotachi, considered a female deity, and the right foot was Kuni no Tokotachi, the male deity who was born in a reed according to the *Nihon Shoki*. No matter what terminology is used to explain this process, it refers to uniting the body. Everything must be one. This is the central principle in this technique, in tenchinage, and in all aikido waza in general.

After performing this exercise, we all sat down on the mat in a circle around the master, and he began talking. We recorded this lecture:

Everything becomes clear with the development of the spirit. For as long as I continue my life in this world, I hope to work toward establishing a true Aikido for the benefit of this world. There is no Aikido separate from me. Everything is based on the su [essence] of the Divine Breath. The universe itself is the solidification of this essence. This is why I originally set out in the pursuit of studying ki, knowledge, and virtue. It is still the reason I continue to train and study. Aikido is the divine practice of Odo. First, it is necessary to begin by standing on the Ame no Ukihashi

[Floating Bridge of Heaven]. Having one's feet on the Ame no Ukihashi, you must understand that A means to be completely natural. Me means to move. Ame then means to move around freely and flow naturally. This is like water. Combining water with fire moves the water, so water and steam is put to use by fire. Instruction must always follow this principle. I have achieved this with iki [life]. From this comes kokyu [breath]. When one breathes in, one's spirit flows in as well. Breath can freely be removed by ki.

To complete the circle and make it perfect, to know the center of the circle is the first step toward Ai: love and harmony. To stand always at the center of centers is to stand on the spirit of the world forming process. In order to avoid conflict one takes steps beforehand to avert a fight. This is the function of true Budo. At the heart of this is the way of love. The way of love is the power and life of this world. It is also very important to use the spirit and the eyes. A conflict should not arise if one continues spiritual training, because this training is life itself. Aikido also serves as a way of maintaining good health and physical beauty, overcoming obstacles and promoting good manners. Aikido should always promote good manners. Good manners are the expression of love and tolerance. Bad manners have no place in spiritual training. Aikido is true Budo and spiritual training.

O-Sensei obviously viewed Aikido as a spiritual pursuit, and it is tempting for many students to jump into the spiritual realm. However, it is important to remember that O-Sensei only recognized the spiritual dimensions of the art after decades of training in the physical techniques. There is no way to skip steps. Just train hard, and eventually, a spiritual component will naturally appear. The focus must be on the physical techniques. To train ineffectively in the hope of gaining some kind of spiritual awakening is a delusion. Aikido is a martial art of attack and defense. Any art that does not have efficient, deadly techniques is not Budo. It is a fraud.

Training needs to be safe, but the techniques should be applied effectively. It takes skill and experience to balance this. In time, the martial arts, which on the surface are arts used to maim and kill, become spiritual. The deadly techniques that can destroy others now become the means to protect and serve. Truly, concepts like the death-dealing sword and the life-giving blade are found within the same traditions. The former is initially apparent, while the latter develops slowly, and it will only develop through incessant training.

65. Zen Staff

CHAPTER 19:
THE POWER OF HUMILITY

66. Donn Draeger demonstrating tai sabaki kote in Tokyo.

*W*hile I was in Japan, O-Sensei did not spend all of his time at the Hombu Dojo. He taught a couple times weekly, and he was at the Iwama Dojo occasionally. Most of the classes that I attended were taught by his son Ueshiba Kisshomaru, Okumura Shigenobu, or other shihan. When I was not at the dojo, I traveled around and learned as much as I could about

Japan. I visited calligraphy teachers and exhibits. I also headed over to the Judo Hombu Dojo, the Kodokan, and trained. Occasionally, I also trained at one of Tomiki Kenji's dojo, one of O-Sensei's first eighth-dans. Initially a Judo practitioner, he began learning Daito-ryu Aikijujutsu from O-Sensei in 1926, and was given a teaching scroll in 1940. He taught at the Hombu Dojo during the 1950s, and eventually created his own style of Aikido, which combined the competitive element of Judo with the physical techniques of Aikido. I also met the *soke dairi* of Katori Shinto-ryu, and met up with Donn Draeger at a demonstration. In addition, I studied sword with Hakusui Inami and practiced a little *kyudo*, Japanese archery. I also enjoyed going shopping for antiques and visiting sword shops. Even after O-Sensei died, I continued to return to Japan to shop for antiques and swords.

One time, Meik Skoss, who started his training in our San Fernando Dojo, and I went to the *Toranomon* area of Tokyo to visit a sword shop. At the time, he was studying under Yagyu, who was famous, the inheritor of the Yagyu Shinkage-ryu tradition. Since his instructor was famous, he thought that he would mention his name, so that the owner of the shop would recognize us as experts and show us the finest merchandise. However, I asked him to let me do the talking, and he agreed. We started looking around at the things on display, including *tsuba* and different types of blades. But as everyone knows about Japanese sword shops, the best merchandise is never on display. The owner was watching us, and he eventually came over and asked, "Do you know a lot about swords?"

"No," I replied. I don't know much, but I am interested. I actually knew your father."

He did not think this was possible, as his father had died years before, so I told him about the sword that I had asked his father to service. It was forged by Rai Kunimitsu, a famous fourteenth-century swordsmith from Fujishiro. Some of his blades are today considered national treasures. All sword polishers keep records about the swords that they work on, and since this was a rather famous smith, I knew that he could verify what I had told him. He disappeared into the back room for a bit, and when he returned, he acknowledged that his father had in fact worked on one of my swords. He then asked, "Would you like to see some really great swords?"

Of course, I said yes, and Meik and I were permitted to get into an elevator with him, which took us to the penthouse upstairs, where the real collection was displayed. I was amazed seeing the items that he had, and I was even more amazed when he pulled out a naginata, which was crafted by one of the top swordsmith in Japanese history. I am not a huge fan of naginata, but it was designated a national treasure by the Japanese government. It was beautiful. I asked about swords, and he pulled out another national treasure, a sword, followed by five other blades that had been classified as important cultural properties. It was all incredible.

I am certain that we were only shown these special items because I said I did not know anything, yet expressed an interest (in learning more). A test some owners use is the following: they ask if you know a lot about swords. If you say yes, they will say something like, "Ok. Let me show you a really nice blade," and they pull out a good forgery. If you cannot determine that it is fake, you will not be shown anything more, and chances are, you will never even know that your ignorance had been discovered. If you did not recognize it as fake, that would be the end of it. We gained the advantage in Japan by saying that we knew nothing. This lesson should not be forgotten. Humility can give you an advantage.

Unfortunately, humility does not increase over time in the martial arts. It is just the opposite. Ranking seems to slowly erode modesty, and students train hard to get a black belt. Once they get it, they believe that they are good, that they have nothing else to learn. Some potential students have dropped by my dojo before and asked, "How long does it take to get a black belt?" Obviously, they could pick up a catalogue and order one at any time. I have never understood this fascination with colored belts. Originally, time and use darkened a belt. And even when it did become dark, a different shade, it was not indicative of the owner's skill level. Some people think that rank is synonymous with skill, and that a certain colored belt enables them to teach. A woman once called my dojo:

She asked if I was looking for instructors. She seemed professional, focused, and forthright, asking about class times, student attendance, and other instructor related details.

"How long have you been studying Aikido?" I asked.

"I haven't," she said. "But I have studied a bit of Karate and I have taught Yoga and aerobics."

"If you haven't studied Aikido," I said, "why are you calling about teaching positions?"

"I'm a quick learner," she said. "I think I can pick it up quickly."

"Oh really?" I said. "You'll need about fifteen years to gain a slight understanding. Fifth-degree black belt is the first instructor rank."

"So you are not looking for instructors?" she replied.

"Not right now," I responded.

My students often tell me how students of other arts are overwhelmed at the length of time for an Aikido black belt. They also assume that it is an instructor's rank. It is not. It marks a serious student who has a firm understanding of the basic techniques, and who can now begin real training. Aikido is not simply gross motor skills. It contains a series of internal processes that transcend simple techniques. You cannot just "pick it up." It cannot be bought, stolen, borrowed, or faked. It requires committed and rigorous training over many years. There are no shortcuts. Just train. Always remain humble and maintain a beginner's mind.

Humility can lead to progress, so get rid of the ego, and train as though you were seeing techniques for the first time. It is possible that you are seeing techniques for the first time, although they might look exactly like previously practiced techniques to the unobservant student. This is what distinguishes a good student from a poor one. Good students are more observant, and they watch their instructors perform techniques as though they were seeing them for the first time, even though they might have seen them hundreds of times before. Good students are looking for the small changes, the hidden body movements. Poor students just assume that they have seen it before and there is nothing else to be gained from watching it again. When O-Sensei demonstrated a technique, I paid close attention. I wanted to see everything that he was demonstrating, so I approached practice like a beginner. This mindset, which is heralded by Zen, opens your mind to more instruction. Once it is open, you can perceive more. You begin to see the details. A famous story about the tea master Sen no Rikyu illustrates this mindset:

He had asked a carpenter to hang a flower vase on the tearoom wall, and he was driving the man crazy. Seated on the tatami, he kept telling him things like "more left," "higher," "lower," "more right," until he had found the perfect spot. The carpenter believed that the tea master was just being difficult, and that there was no way he could tell if the vase was hung where he marked it, instead of a centimeter or two off the spot. To test him, the carpenter secretly marked the spot and then pretended to have lost it. He asked Sen no Rikyu to guide him to the correct location again. After the same prodding, the carpenter was eventually guided back to the exact same spot. It was at this point that he realized how perfect the tea master's concentration was. His attention to detail was phenomenal. And this is what makes a great student in the martial arts or in any other discipline. When beginning to learn the art of calligraphy, many practice the single stroke for *ichi*, the number one, repeatedly, trying to duplicate the brush stroke of their master. Poor students might look at it and see a single line, while good students will see variations in the stroke caused by the individual hairs of the brush, the pressure changes of the hand that held the brush, and so on. If you approach any field of study as though you were a beginner, you can eventually become a master.

A Zen teaching is: "Always maintain a beginner's mind." It is only by maintaining this mind that students can truly remain open to instruction. My teacher, Takahashi Isao, once duplicated an old and trite martial teaching in my home. I think just about every martial art student has heard this one before: the tale about the overflowing teacup. I do not know where this story actually began, as it has been repeated so many times, but somewhere, at some time, a master was pouring tea for his student, and he kept pouring so that the cup overflowed. The student, thinking his instructor mad, asked, "What are you doing?"

The instructor replied, "This cup, like your mind, is full. Nothing more will go in. If you wish to learn, you must first empty your cup."

This story has been overused, and I do not like seeing it in books, but my teacher actually did this to me. We were in my living room, drinking tea, and our cups were resting on the red lacquer table that I thought Mori Sensei had scratched when cutting a phone book in half. I really like that table, so I hoped my instructors would teach me lessons away from it, not using it. But Takahashi Sensei overflowed my cup, and I was worried about its surface. It did not occur to me that he was replaying this simple teaching. I asked what he was doing, and he repeated the same trite lines that I had heard so many times before. At the time, I was perturbed, but then I started thinking about it. This teaching has been around for a long time, and perhaps the reason it continues to be used is that the analogy between the mind and the teacup is apt.

Although I had experienced many situations that should have made me humble, such as being thrown by a girl on the streets of Paris, being tossed around by people in various dojo who were wearing white belts, and being defeated by a swordsman with a broom, I was still full of myself. I had not yet learned humility. I thought I was a great martial artist, and that trophy telling me that I was a Judo champion did not help. It only reinforced my ego. After this teacup incident, I decided to embrace humility and behave as though I were a beginner. (This was not just for me, but also for the sake of my poor table!) I took off my black belt and put on a white one. Since then, for over fifty years, I have continued to wear my white belt. When training in Japan, I also wore a white belt. O-Sensei did the same. He had no rank, yet he was great.

The confident and yet gentle presence of mature warriors is always surprising. With no need to prove themselves, they walk freely through both calm times and dangerous situations as though there were no difference between the two. The practice of Aikido accords with Zen practice. Both demand that the individual take full responsibility for life, carrying nothing into each new moment, ready and awake for the challenge of the eternal "now." Like Zen, Aikido is a life practice, and even first-time practitioners feel the benefits of training for mind and body development. The spirit and the mind are the heart of both Aikido and Zen. What is the self being defended in self-defense? What is the sword that is Aikido? Polish this sword in severe and endless training, and the true self will emerge.

67. Persimmons (Sumi-e), after Mu Qi

CHAPTER 20:
ANOTHER LECTURE BY THE FOUNDER

*D*uring the last decade of O-Sensei's life, he worked hard to spread Aikido throughout not just Japan, but the entire world. When he traveled to Hawaii in 1961 to support the opening of the Hawaii Aikido Dojo, he explained:

> *The reason for my visit to Hawaii is to build a "silver bridge" between Hawaii and Japan. In Japan, we have already built some "golden bridges" – it is time now to build bridges across the ocean, so with my visit, I want to link East and West through Aikido. Aikido's role is to link the world together through harmony and love. I am still in the midst of my own training, and so I feel not only the need to build such bridges but also to continue polishing the true way of Budo. Through a true Budo, such as Takemusu Aiki, we must create harmony for all of humanity, and envelop all creation in universal love.[42]*

When he returned, he continued to perform demonstrations and raise public awareness of the art that he had created. In 1964, he received an honorary medal from the Emperor called the Order of the Rising Sun for his efforts in the martial arts. After, O-Sensei spent more time in Tokyo. He never lost interest in farming, and he seemingly still liked the dojo at Iwama, but he spent most of his time at the Tokyo dojo. It was decided that the dojo would be updated; a new building would be built. A Shinto ceremony was held to bless the site of the new building on March 14, 1967, and construction began on the same day. O-Sensei himself led the way by plowing the ground. Construction was completed ten months later, on December 15. A ceremony was held on January 12, 1968 to commemorate the new dojo's completion. Some shihan from Hombu Dojo demonstrated techniques, which functioned as a preface to O-Sensei's own demonstration. After, he addressed the crowd and said, "I strive to make my Aikido selfless and to expect nothing in return. I pray for the immortality of Aikido. I am working as hard as if I were a living deity."[43]

He held other demonstrations while I was in Japan, including the All-Japan Aikido Demonstration, held on October 5, 1968 in Hibiya Hall. He wore a white hakama, as he sometimes did, and mesmerized the crowd with his techniques and spiritual explanations. In the dojo, he continued to teach us about Aikido. Sometimes the explanations were so complicated that even today I am working on understanding them completely. Aikido is multi-layered, so it is more difficult to understand than some other arts, which might only focus on physical techniques. Nevertheless, we recorded many of the lectures that O-Sensei gave during class. The following is one of them:

Aikido is not for beating others or winning battles. Aikido is based on non-resistance, where there is neither conflict nor victory. Aikido assists all of us to succeed in our respective missions, [which have been] granted to us all by heaven. From the Masakatsu, Agatsu, Katsu Hayabi, at the beginning of this spiritual training process, we progress toward the natural state of universal motions. Training must be continued until right and good are known, until the right and the good of the self are realized. Because they are heaven itself, the people of heaven do not understand that they are in heaven. The purpose of shugyo training is the unification of man and the divine. Man and God are of the same essence, yet vary in magnitude. Man cannot thus supersede his limits. The spirit of Bu is nevertheless capable of producing fully beautiful results when working in accordance with both heaven and earth. Bu is the way of infinite physical change. Holding onto one, it reaches ten thousand. Opening not one but ten thousand laws, it refines the sword of Kusanagi while completing its work. Capable of withstanding any hardship, the heart remains as clear as the sky, as broad as the ocean, and as grand as the mountains. The spirit of Bu gives life to all that are alive, both large and small. You should devote yourself to practice. Experience light and heat and complete yourself as a manifestation of the truth. Further training will strengthen your body and soul and produce an individual in harmony with the laws of nature. Spread Aiki so we can see the full light of the spirit of Aikido shine forth. It goes without saying that the essence of what I have said is that you should strive toward this end. Do that, while at the same time paying close attention to the times in which you live and contribute to the making of a beautiful, pure land.

Some of the points mentioned in this lecture can be traced to Omoto-kyo, the religious or spiritual aspect of Aikido as perceived by the founder. The last line, in particular, echoes the desire of Omoto-kyo leaders to establish a heavenly kingdom on earth. Another line, indicating that human beings do not know that they are heavenly because they are actually in heaven, is related. It points to an important generalized truth as well: It is difficult for human beings to see themselves. This ability to see oneself and one's surroundings clearly must be developed through spiritual, meditative training. O-Sensei explained this: "You should devote yourself to practice. Experience light and heat and complete yourself as a manifestation of the truth. Further training will strengthen your body and soul and produce an individual in harmony with the laws of nature."

Tenchijin, or heaven, earth, and man, is an ancient practice, possibly originating in India. It is found in Chinese and Japanese (internal) martial arts, and it can be interpreted in various ways. It is a Japanese translation of a training method in Chinese internal martial arts, but it is herein used in a metaphysical sense. He said, "The purpose of shugyo training is the unification of man and the divine. Man and God are of the same essence, yet vary in magnitude. Man cannot thus supersede his limits." The purpose of training is so that human beings can realize their divine essence. This is a teaching found in many world religions. As adherents meditate and engage in austerities, they eventually come to realize that the divine is not somewhere else, but it is within each one of us. Enlightenment is nothing more than realizing our own inner nature. A Zen expression states, "This very mind is Buddha." However, it is difficult to understand this. An emperor was studying Zen under a master named Gudo. One day, he asked about this expression. He asked, "Is it true that this mind is Buddha?"

Gudo replied, "If I say yes, you will think you understand what you do not understand. If I say no, I am contradicting something that others know to be true."

It takes discipline and training to understand such things, and according to the founder, that training is Bu. The more you train in Aikido or other martial arts, if you approach the training in the correct manner, you will begin to understand spiritual matters. In this way, the martial arts are moving meditation. To engage in this learning process, students must empty their cups and approach each day anew. They must always maintain a beginner's mind. Once they have this mentality, they must have the will to succeed. It has been said that just refusing to retreat from something provides additional strength. "Masakatsu, Agatsu, Katsu hayabi" [True victory is self-victory. Let that day arrive quickly.] sums up the proper mindset to understand everything. If you can conquer yourself through training, you begin to understand not just your own divine nature, but the nature of those things that surround you. A famous Zen story relates to this:

> A monk asked Seijo: "I understand that a Buddha who lived before recorded history sat in meditation for ten cycles of existence and could not realize the highest truth, and so could not become fully emancipated. Why is this so?"
>
> Seijo replied, "Your question is self-explanatory."
>
> The monk asked, "Since the Buddha was meditating, why could he not fulfill Buddhahood?"
>
> Seijo said, "He was not a Buddha."[44]

He could not attain enlightenment because he was not enlightened. It does not matter how long one meditates. Without this awakening, one will never succeed. It is the same in martial studies. Some students can train for years, going to class three or four times weekly, and yet at the end of years, they have made little progress. These people think that progress will naturally come in time, but this is not true. Good students approach each class as though it were new. They do not care about gain or loss, winning or losing, and gradually they learn how to relax. They watch their instructors' movements closely, trying to perceive even the smallest details. Then, they go home and meditate upon what they had learned, so it becomes a part of them. These people improve, and these students might one day surpass their teachers. Another Zen story can help to clarify this:

> Tozan went to Ummon. Ummon asked him where he had come from.
>
> Tozan said, "From Sato village."
>
> Ummon asked, "In what temple did you remain for the summer?"
>
> Tozan replied, "The temple of Hoji, south of the lake."
>
> "When did you leave there?" asked Ummon, wondering how long Tozan would continue with such factual answers.
>
> "The twenty-fifth of August," answered Tozan.
>
> Ummon said, "I should give you three blows with a stick, but today I forgive you."
>
> The next day Tozan bowed to Ummon and asked, "Yesterday you forgave me three blows. I do not know why you thought me wrong."
>
> Ummon, rebuking Tozan's spiritless responses, said: "You are good for nothing. You simply wander from one monastery to another."
>
> Before Ummon's words were ended, Tozan was enlightened.[45]

As this story indicates, people can train superficially for years with no progress whatsoever. True progress requires a different kind of realization and intent.

Playing my Flute
I stop the World.

Sando.

68. The Shakuhachi

CHAPTER 21:
THE IMPORTANCE OF EFFECTIVE TECHNIQUES

O-Sensei said that physical techniques are a gateway to the spiritual dimension. It therefore makes sense to try to master the art's physical forms. People can philosophize about the theory and spirit of a martial art, but this is not important if the philosophy did not evolve from techniques. In traditional Budo, the underlying philosophy is embodied in techniques that can be executed accurately, effectively, and creatively. In Aikido, the basic techniques of ude-osae, kote-hineri, kote-mawashi, shiho-nage, irimi-nage, kaiten-nage, and kote-gaeshi are, at the same time, simple yet sophisticated. They are difficult to comprehend and to perform perfectly. Beginners naturally find it difficult to replicate even the basic shape of the techniques, including the correct posture and footwork. In time, this becomes easier, but then a new realm of understanding manifests. There is a seemingly unending succession of realms – different layers of meaning. The techniques, then, do not become any easier as practitioners train.

Regarding the physical motions themselves, and the anatomical reasons that they work, repeated practice can help students to improve. That is why Aikido is practiced the way it is, with the instructor demonstrating techniques, and the students practicing them repeatedly. They partner up, one doing the technique (nage), the other receiving it (uke). At the beginning stage of training, uke does not resist, so that nage can explore the movements and gain insights. Eventually, students progress beyond this point, and they learn how to use the techniques in actual fighting. This second stage is only possible through repeated practice, in which uke is compliant. However, repeated practice also makes the range of possibilities wider, and it becomes more difficult for relatively new students, (those who have been practicing for ten years or less), to discern which techniques are correct and which ones are incorrect. In other words, techniques can be performed in inexhaustibly different ways, but all of the variations, if performed correctly, must adhere to the art's underlying principles. In this respect, it is always interesting to watch techniques performed by higher dan-grades and shihan.

You will notice (sometimes with confusion) that all techniques are done differently. Each person who has trained for a long time eventually begins to internalize the techniques. When they are expressed, they are personal expressions. They demonstrate the spirit and understanding of the practitioner, just as brushstrokes in painting or calligraphy reveal an artist's state of being. It is possible to execute the same exact technique in different ways, while remaining true to the underlying philosophy that makes the techniques work. This same philosophy also makes the techniques part of a specific style. In other words, a technique like ude-osae exists in just about every martial art on the planet. Nevertheless, when I watch people performing this arm-bar technique, I can instantly tell if they train in Judo, Brazilian Jujutsu, Sambo, Daito-ryu Aikijujutsu, or other arts. This same technique is performed differently in all the arts, and all variants are effective. However, no matter how differently advanced Aikido students perform the technique, the variations are always recognized as Aikido. This is because the underlying concepts are always maintained. Perhaps this is why O-Sensei said that there are unlimited techniques in Aikido. He just borrowed techniques from Daito-ryu, which he used to express the underlying philosophy of Aikido.

After training in the physical dimension of the art's techniques for years, another naturally opens. The practice of Aikido is a practical exploration of the limits to one's self-discipline, personal principles, and self-awareness in relation to others. This personal dimension is essential to Aikido, whether it is in the relationship with one's instructor, or the (usually different) relationship with other dojo members.

The execution of techniques at a satisfactory level is a never-ending process. It can take years to perform them correctly. However, the more students try to imitate their instructor's techniques the more they come to realize that imitation is not the correct description of what actually occurs. Imitation seems to imply something that is not creative, yet even if the imitation was a faithful replica of the instructor's techniques, it would still be different. This is because each person has a different body. The techniques will naturally be personalized. An exact replica of the instructor's techniques would not have much value, because nothing should ever remain the same. O-Sensei always said, "Today's techniques will be different tomorrow. Do not get caught up in form and appearance."

Imitation is, of course, an essential teaching device, especially for the acquisition of physical and mental discipline, but it takes many years of repeated practice to begin to be aware of what is actually occurring when practicing Aikido. Even then, it is by no means certain that this awareness can be expressed adequately in words or taught to other people. To perform Aikido correctly, one must be creative. In one sense, this is what the founder meant when he referred to Takemusu Aiki.

69. O-Sensei in front of the kamiza. The large sword was supposedly given to him by Takeda Sokaku. When I visited Aizu Wakamatsu Castle, I saw several large swords like this. It seems that the Takeda samurai liked big swords. Leaning on the wall is a Su-yari (spear).

In any ideological movement founded by an individual with remarkable physical and spiritual gifts, such as O-Sensei, a problem arises. It becomes difficult for followers to figure out how to capture the physical and spiritual bequests of the founder while remaining within the confines of the style. It should be possible for someone who had never known or been taught by the founder to touch his charisma through one of his disciples and become yet another link in a chain, which brings about the next generation of practitioners without loss of truth or spirit. Aikido is not the first art that has had to solve this problem, nor will it be the last. The art is also facing organizational problems while, at the same time, Japan is facing problems of internationalization. The parallels are clear. They cannot be ignored. It will be interesting to see how much of its essential "Japanese-ness" and how much of the truth of O-Sensei's teachings is retained as it adapts itself to the demands of the twenty-first century and countries throughout the world. We must make sure that Aikido is practiced in a way that is congruent with what O-Sensei taught.

To remain true to O-Sensei's teachings, one should concentrate on the style's basic techniques. Remember that O-Sensei was one of the top martial artists in the entire country. Many people came to challenge him, including high-ranking practitioners of other arts and members of the Armed Forces. By all accounts, he defeated them all, and many of his defeated challengers became his students. Strive to maintain the martial element of the art by training in physical techniques. Eventually the spiritual component will develop.

The technical roots of Aikido are in Daito-ryu Aikijujutsu, so a true student should also explore this art. How else could one fully understand the principles behind the techniques as learned by O-Sensei from his teacher Takeda Sokaku? Think of Aikido as a flower. To keep the techniques effective and beautiful, you must understand and care for the roots. Otherwise, the flower will be like silk or plastic fake flowers that one occasionally sees collecting dust in the corner of a waiting room or hotel lobby. They have no roots. They are mere imitations. Strive to understand the genius of Daito-ryu techniques. Then, learn about the belief system that O-Sensei referred to, which is found in the Omoto-kyo faith. It is only in this way that one can truly understand the art.

I cannot stress enough that your techniques must be martially effective. Effectiveness cannot be discarded for imitative spiritual practices. The true spiritual practices in Aikido are within the performance of hard, effective techniques. O-Sensei was known as one of the greatest fighters in modern Japanese history, and his art was originally characterized by powerful strikes to the opponent's weak points, throws which allowed no possibility of uke protecting himself, and extremely painful joint locks. After defeating many incomers, people started to understand that he was a man to be reckoned with. They began to fear his martial prowess. Eventually, they hesitated to challenge him, because of his power.

When carrying on the Aikido tradition, we must be careful that the martial efficacy never wanes. In Daito-ryu today, properly applied techniques allow the opponent no possibility to take ukemi. All techniques will result in the opponent being either maimed or killed. These same techniques were modified for use in Aikido. Many of the techniques in Aikido are friendlier, and they provide ways for people to defend themselves against them. This leads to the possibility of sport applications. Kano Jigoro eliminated the deadly techniques of jujutsu styles so that they could be performed safely in a sport application. Likewise, O-Sensei made the techniques of Daito-ryu less martially effective so that they could be safely trained and used for a different purpose, that of spreading peace. For this reason, modern practitioners must never forget the original forms, so that the art does not go the way of karate, Judo, and other sports that are in the Olympics. O-Sensei said:

> From ancient times, Budo has never been considered a sport. If there are contests, we must be ready to kill. Those who seek competition are making a grave mistake. To smash, injure, or destroy is the worst sin a human being can commit. The old saying, "The martial deities never kill" is true. Real Budo is a Path of Peace.[46]

Someone once asked me why Aikido is not as popular as some other sports. I explained that it is not a sport. It is not entertainment, and it is definitely not just a fun way to pass your time if you have nothing else to do. It is a way to train your mind and spirit, and it forces you to face yourself and confront what you are seeing. This is not easy for many people, for if you do not like what you see, you are now forced to change it. This change is not easy. The entire process of training in traditional Budo is a self-realization and self-changing experience. There are no excuses. You cannot blame anybody or anything for your lack of discipline or inefficiency. This is not a popular idea in our times. People tend to want a way out. If they are not good at something or have difficulty concentrating, they like to blame it on something else. This mentality holds no place in traditional Budo. Once you have dedicated yourself to this path, there is no escape. O-Sensei taught this:

> *The martial arts of our country are not called sports. The purpose of martial arts is to shape and perfect ourselves. Once we build ourselves up, we have to realize everything successfully and as human beings, must protect all nature. In our country, originally, we do not have such sports as people have in Western countries. Some people are delighted to say that the Japanese martial arts have gained in popularity since they became sports. However, this is a gross misunderstanding that shows they do not know at all what the Japanese martial arts really are. Sports are games and pastimes that do not involve the spirit. They are competitions only between physical bodies and not between souls. Thus, they are competitions merely for the sake of pleasure. The Japanese martial arts are a competition in how we can express and realize love that unites and protects everything in harmony and helps this world to prosper.[47]*

Traditional Budo provides a means to discover oneself. The more you train, the more you realize who you are. You begin to recognize the ego, and you see the ego as your own enemy. In this way, the self is recognized as an enemy. By deconstructing the self, one begins to understand reality. Intellectual understanding is not sufficient. Only by hard and serious training, called shugyo in Japanese, can we hope to achieve this goal. The founder said, "Aikido is not for beating others or winning battles. It is for developing your spirit. Everything becomes clear with the development of the spirit. Within the very techniques there is deep meaning." This is unlike learning a trick or a clever way to do something. To discover these meanings and face yourself means to enter a dojo and train wholeheartedly. It is much different from attending school or going to a gym.

It involves a pledge between teacher and student. Instruction is always imparted directly, face to face. It is imparted mind to mind, like the Buddha's Flower Sermon. Instruction is imparted from teacher to student in a traditional manner that has been proven effective because it has survived for centuries. The relationship between a martial art instructor and his or her students is not like that between a club member and an aerobics instructor. It is more like the relationship that exists between a parent and a child. This is how a martial arts instructor was traditionally perceived in Japan.

Although Aikido is a Budo and teaches people how to react when attacked, it is more importantly a way of training the body and developing the spirit. If your training is lax, you will not have great results. A proper attitude and approach is essential. Train as hard as you can, and all the petty stuff will fall away. Your priorities will be correct. Your competence in other parts of your life will improve, and you will spend less energy and mental focus on irrelevant things.

The way you train is the way you live.

The way you live is the way you train.

These are not two separate things. You are one.

70. The Sacred Sounds of Kotodama

CHAPTER 22:
KOTODAMA

O-Sensei always spoke and wrote about *kotodama*, a term that means "word spirits" or "word souls." When he used the term, he generally pronounced it as kototama, (using a devoiced /t/ sound instead of /d/, which is not a standard Japanese pronunciation). Kotodama is a complex phenomenon, and it is generally seen in the new Shinto-based religions, such as Kurozumi-kyo, Omoto-kyo, and Byakko Shinko-kai. The term describes the theory that every sound creates energy. When a sound is uttered, the vibratory energy created can help to awaken one's understanding of spiritual phenomena. This idea is not unique to Japan. It is possible that it originated in India, but the concept is also found in Western religions. In Christianity, for example, there is the idea of *logos*. In the beginning, there was the Word, the Word was with God, and all things came into being through the Word. This is the same concept: the universe began with a vibration. This vibration can be accessed through sound. However, it is a mistake to think that the audible sounds are the most important part of kotodama.

Shirata Rinjiro (1912-1993) was a powerful prewar student of O-Sensei. He trained back when Hombu Dojo was called the Kobukan. Colloquially, it was called "hell dojo." He was also a follower of Omoto-kyo, the same religion upon which O-Sensei fixated, so his understanding of kotodama principles is beneficial. He explained:

> *Kotodama is not sounds. It is the echo of ki, which precedes the emergence of sounds. Sounds are the next stage. Kotodama comes first, and preceding it, there is ki. Ki changes into many forms. It becomes sound, light, and kokyu. When two sources of ki combine, this results in kokyu. While breathing, it becomes sound, light, kotodama, and many other things. And it becomes hibiki [echoes], that is, the seventy-five sounds. Subtle changes of hibiki become the mystery of creation. First, there was the Word and the Word was God – this is kotodama and also aiki.*[48]

Considering the phenomenon in this way, it is easy to see why the founder considered kotodama important. It is related to kokyu and ki, and it can create energy. The founder believed the seed syllable of the entire universe was "U," which gave birth to "SU." O-Sensei said:

> The kototama of "U" is the form of eternal prosperity within nothingness – no heaven, no earth, only the expanse of the infinite vacuum. From within this oneness comes the first spark of life and consciousness. From that point, infinitesimal particles of ki radiating life energy begin to map out a larger circle around this first spark. The result is the kototama of "SU," the beginningless beginning of the universe. The biblical expression "In the beginning was the Word" refers to this kototama. When one understands the working of spiral energy and trains oneself in the truth of the spirit, aiki is created.[49]

This initial sound, which later gave birth to all things, is often represented by a circle with a dot in the center of it. Sometimes, O-Sensei replaced the dot with the *katakana* "SU."

This vibratory energy continued and morphed into the other vowel sounds, which are called mother sounds. The "I" sound is thought by believers to unite heaven and earth, and it therefore relates directly to Aikido techniques like tenchinage, and its philosophy of tenchijin, "heaven, earth, and human beings." The "A" sound infers expansion. The individual energy within each person is the same as the universal energy. The temporary form it resides in, our bodies, give the false impression that each person is separate. But according to belief systems that make use of kotodama practices, everything is actually connected. This is because the energy within each person stemmed from, and is connected to, the universal ki. By voicing this sound and initiating the vibrations associated with it, practitioners can become more aware of this connection. Martially, it can make them stronger, as they become aware of an unlimited source of power.

The vibratory energy of "E" prevents the energy within our bodies from stagnating. Consider flowing water versus stagnant water. The idea behind some East Asian medical practices, including acupressure, acupuncture, and *kiatsu*, is that ki can stagnate. When it does, people get sick. To fix this stagnating energy, acupuncture doctors use needles, acupressure experts stimulate the pressure points of the body using physical compression, while kiatsu practitioners use their own energy to stimulate the energy flow in another.

The "O" energy stimulates the cerebellum and temporal lobe, and intoning the sound can increase ki power. All of these mother sounds work together, and it is impossible to separate them. Making it even more complicated is that they rarely function alone. They combine with father sounds. The so-called father sounds are the consonants. They are the vibratory energies that are more simply defined in terms of yin and yang. When the consonants and the vowels combine, they spur creation.

When O-Sensei intoned kotodama, he usually did the following:

1. First, he intoned the kotodama of creation once:
   SU – U – U – U – U – YU – MU.

2. Next, he repeated the kotodama of existence three times:
   A – O – U – E – I.

3. He said, MASAKATSU, AGATSU, KATSUHAYABI once.
   This translates to "True victory is self-victory. Let that day arrive quickly."

4. Then, AIKI O-KAMI (the Great Spirit of Aiki) was said once.

5. O-Sensei would then return to the saying MASAKATSU, AGATSU, KATSUHAYABU, and intone the sounds that make up the words thirteen times.

6. Lastly, he would say the following expression thirteen times:
   NAMU AME NO MURAKUMO KUKI SAMUHARA RYUUOO.

Namu means something like "I take refuge in," and it is often heard among Buddhists in such expressions as *"namu amida butsu."* Ame is heaven. Murakumo translates to "gathering clouds." However, the terms together (Ame no Murakumo) refers to the sword Ame no Murakumo no Tsurugi, also known as Kusanagi. It is one of the three Imperial Regalia: sword, mirror, and jewel. *Kuki* literally translates as "nine demons," but has been translated by others as "nine fierce spirits." *Samuhara* is "cold plain." Finally, *ryu-oo* translates to "Dragon King." When put together, this is the name of a deity that O-Sensei believed possessed him. He saw himself as this Dragon King and even had a scroll made in which he was depicted as such.

O-Sensei explained how kotodama relates to Aikido:

Aikido is the Way of the principle of the eternal, unchanging system of the Universe. The Great Emptiness was created before the birth of the universal "SU" voice, the One Original Source (ichigen), our parent God. Life is the history of the acts of God since then, since the ancient age of deities of our country, and the practices of Aikido originate in this history. My Aikido is a Way to perform ascetic practices guided by Divine Providence while expressing the significance of the Divine Sword (katsuragi) and being a manifestation of the sword itself. I regard it as the true martial art (bujutsu). The workings of the universe are called "takemusu aiki," and are born from the One Original Source and unify water and fire, that is, the Breath of Heaven and the Breath of Earth in order to produce one unified breath. I would like to explain what this means. When the soul and body bestowed upon me interact with each other as an inseparable union through the workings of "SU" and "U," I produce the voices "A, O, U, E, I" from the bottom of my abdomen, letting them emanate from my physical mouth. This form is exactly the same as the manifestation of the frictional actions produced by the movements of water and fire, that is, the interactions of the two deities Takami Musubi and Kami Musubi, when they dance while ascending spirally to the right and descending spirally to the left. If we polish and perfect kotodama, the spirit given to each one of us and which is our true nature, all explanations concerning every combination of all things and the wisdom to understand the true state of the Great Creation of this world will be given to us.[50]

Kotodama is confusing, even for experts on world religions. Some Aikido practitioners today do not even consider this aspect of the art. They train in the physical techniques alone, and they claim to be following the teachings of O-Sensei. But the only way that we can approach the understanding that O-Sensei had is to consider his teachings seriously: all of them, not just the ones that we can easily understand. Today, there is a tendency to disregard anything that is not easily understood, but sometimes, understanding only develops through repetitious practice. I did not initially understand why we did all the specific warm-up exercises that we did. I also did not understand why O-Sensei chanted such seemingly unimportant sounds. In addition, I didn't know why certain techniques were performed the way they were, and I thought of many different ways to accomplish the same result. Nevertheless, I followed my teacher's example. I performed the techniques as I was taught to perform them, and I continued to do the warm-up exercises, breathing exercises, and kotodama chanting. Eventually, I came to understand the genius behind such movements.

One of my old acquaintances, Furuya Kensho, used to describe such a revelation to his students. Like many martial artists, he was interested in artwork, Japanese swords, and the tea ceremony. While performing the tea ceremony, there is a specific order to every move. After scooping some powdered tea into the teacups, the cold-water lid must be removed before removing the hot-water lid. This did not seem to make much sense to him, since they never used cold water during the ceremonies, so he skipped it. His teacher would constantly remind him to do so, but since it did not make sense to him, he often forgot. Then, years later, he realized why that lid must be removed first. As one becomes proficient in making and serving tea, one is eventually able to sense the proper temperature of the water as it is ladled out. If it is too hot, some cold water must be added before serving it so that it is at the proper temperature. This might not seem like a big deal, but the point is that every motion in traditional arts is likely there for a purpose.

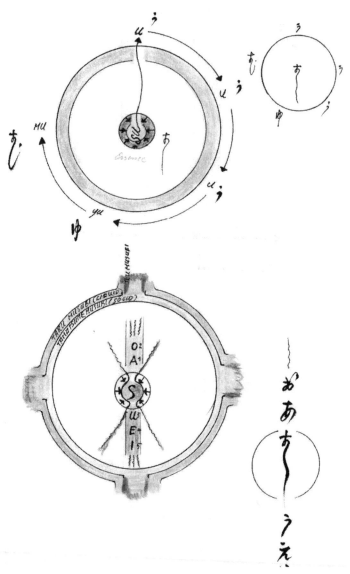

71. Diagram of Kotodama Theory

This is especially true with the martial arts. The old arts that survived to the present day survived because they are superior. During the Warring States Period, warriors with inferior techniques went out to the battlefield and never came home. Those with good techniques killed others and returned. Among those, some talented individuals fought in many battles, killed many people, and yet still managed to survive. Others understood that they had serious martial skills, and they wished to train with such people. This began the typical student-teacher relationship that is found in martial arts today. The techniques that these Budo geniuses used were codified so that they could be taught to others. This is the beginning of the martial ryu. In Zen, it is useless to ask why one sits in a specific way or why one sits at all, as sitting itself will eventually provide the answers. In Rinzai Zen, they used to hit the students with a stick called *kyosaku*. I think they had it right. Train until you realize the significance of the action. As is heard in many martial art dojo, "Shut up and train!"

One look at the A
destroys evil
The efficacy of the mantra
transforms this body into Buddha.

72. The Kotodama A

CHAPTER 23:
MY FINAL MEETING WITH O-SENSEI

*I*n 1969, after having spent two years in Japan training with the founder, I had to return to the United States. The day before I left, I went to O-Sensei's office. I wanted him to sign a photograph for me. One of the senior students, who acted as his secretary, asked what I wanted. After I explained that I wanted an autograph, she brushed me off, saying something like, "He does not have time for that." I persisted, but she did not relent, so eventually, I turned around and headed back to my dorm room. O-Sensei must have asked her what had occurred, and when he found out, he was not happy. I was asked to return to his office, where he not only signed a picture for me, but he also gave me a scroll. It read, "Ame no murakumo kuki samuhara ryu-oo." Since I collect artwork and view him with awe, it was a fantastic gift. I felt honored to have such an item. I thanked him, said my goodbyes, and then got my things together to return to the U.S. I learned later that he died shortly thereafter.

O-Sensei was actually sick the entire time I was in Japan, and although he did not show it, he must have been in tremendous pain each time he stepped onto the mat. He had a terminal case of liver cancer. On March 8, O-Sensei returned to Tokyo from Iwama, and he was ill. Weak and showing signs of jaundice, he remained in bed and said, "The gods are calling me." His personal doctor visited and suggested that he go to see a specialist. While others were planning to take him to the hospital the next day, O-Sensei's indomitable spirit prevailed. Trying to forget his pain, he went to the dojo and trained for the last time. After, his condition quickly worsened. The director of the Aikikai Foundation at the time, Sonoda Sunao, pulled some strings, and a specialist at Kokuritsu Dai-Ichi Hospital examined him. He suggested immediate hospitalization, and another friend, Tomita Yoshinobu, made it happen. O-Sensei was admitted to Keio hospital, where the doctors suggested that he undergo immediate surgery. However, he did not wish to stay in the hospital, and he definitely did not want surgery. He said, "Take me back to the dojo. I will die in the dojo. I cannot be at peace if I am not in the dojo…"[51] On

March 26, the hospital discharged him. In April, his condition deteriorated, and many of his students came to the bedside to visit. O-Sensei turned to all present and said, "Aikido benefits our society and our nation. It is not only yours. Think that you are practicing for the good of the nation and of the world."[52] On April 25, he had a high fever and then slipped into a coma. He died at five a.m. the next day. He was eighty-six years old.

I was upset when I heard the news, as all of his students must have been. He was a remarkable man, and I am so fortunate to have learned from him. I was taught so much while I was in Japan that it took me a long time to assimilate the information. While the Buddha remained at Vaisali for several weeks, making sense out of his experiences, it took me decades to sort through some of the knowledge that I had received. I soon understood that my duty as O-Sensei's student is to carry on the art, as he would have intended, to the best of my abilities. At that point, I dedicated my life to Aikido.

I returned to Hawaii, where my wife Hana and I had established an art business, and I continued to train in Aikido there. Before leaving for Japan, I had trained with Tohei Sensei, but after the founder's death, the political divisions began. Many high-ranking students left Hombu Dojo and came to Europe and North and South America, where they started their own organizations. Tohei Sensei also separated from hombu. He had many reasons for doing so, and it was justified. However, that left me with a problem. If I supported Tohei Sensei, I was unwelcome in any of the dojo under the auspices of Ueshiba Kisshomaru Sensei. If I stayed with the Ueshiba family, I was not welcome in Tohei's dojo. This was not a good situation, and unfortunately, it has gotten even worse with regards to the political situation in Aikido today. I felt a sense of loyalty to the founder and to Ueshiba Kisshomaru Sensei, so I stayed with Hombu Dojo. Because of this political affiliation, I could no longer train with my old teacher, Tohei Sensei. I thought it was the right decision at the time, but looking back on it now, I think I made a mistake. Life went on though, and I trained at Yoshioka Sadao Sensei's Hawaii Aikikai Hombu Dojo through the 1970s and 1980s.

I did not like the political organizations and the conflict that was beginning, as such concerns direct students away from true Aikido. The founder was one of the top martial artists in the country, and it is up to us to carry on the martial tradition that he began. In an effort to wake people up and remind them to truly follow O-Sensei, I gave away the precious scroll that O-Sensei had given me. In December 1979, I offered it to the Hawaii Aikikai Dojo on Waialae Avenue, thinking that they would treasure it. I considered that it would affect more people in the dojo that it would in my own home. They sent me a letter of gratitude, which read:

Dear Dr. Walther von Krenner,

The Hawaii Aiki Kai acknowledges receipt of your donation of one oil painting of the late founder of Aikido, Morihei Ueshiba, and one calligraphy done by the late founder Morihei Ueshiba, circa 1965. These gifts by you, of the late founder of Aikido, greatly enhance the spirit of Aikido in our organization. We are deeply indebted to you and your generous contribution to this organization. Morihei Ueshiba (1883-1969) founded the martial art of Aikido on the premise that "budo" is not a means of felling one's opponent or enemy, but a means of reconciling all men in this world to become one with each other and with the universe. Your generosity exemplifies that you have truly understood this meaning of "budo." We, of the Hawaii Aiki Kai, humbly thank you again and sincerely hope that with people of your stature in this world, the founder's dream can come true soon.

With deep appreciation,

Yamashita Masaji

Shortly after giving this scroll to the dojo, Hana and I moved to Montana, where I thought I could devote myself to Aikido in a manner that the founder would approve. I wanted to get away from the organizations and the politics, so we moved. Many years later, I wrote to the Hawaii Aikikai, requesting a photograph of the scroll. I was shocked when they told me that the scroll was no longer at the dojo. A friend of mine stopped by to investigate, and it was true; it was not there. After talking to various people, the scroll reappeared at the dojo, and no one seemed to know who had brought it in. Since it was back, they were able to honor my request and send me a picture of the calligraphy. When I received it, I was dismayed.

73. The scroll after years of neglect　　**74. The same scroll after restoration**

They had not taken care of it at all. The paper it was brushed upon had yellowed, and it was stained and ripped. Besides the fact that a large calligraphic piece brushed by the founder is extremely valuable, it is also irreplaceable as a work of art. Calligraphy by famous martial artists was always held in high regard in Japan and China, because it was thought that the soul of the artist was revealed in the brushstrokes. As an artist and calligrapher, this notion makes sense to me, which is why it was so shocking to find that the piece had been treated with such utter disregard. The fate of the founder's calligraphy is indicative of what has occurred in the Aikido world since his death.

Some endlessly quote O-Sensei and publicize Aikido virtues, but their speech is empty. They talk about harmony, respect, and gratitude toward one's teachers, but they do not really honor O-Sensei's work or memory. O-Sensei was a human being, just like everyone else. He did remarkable things, but he was neither a god nor an icon. He started his own martial art. He did not join organizations, and he did not go to seminars. He never had any rank, nor was he concerned with it. He trained, right up until the end. He continually tried to better himself and he never thought that he was great. Today, things are different. Few of us who had actually known him are left. Maybe it is because all the old-timers are disappearing that O-Sensei is becoming a symbol of worship, a cult object. Seemingly few of the new Aikido practitioners are trying to understand his words and give them meaning in their own lives. Most of his words have become intellectual quotes and meaningless sayings that are repeated but not understood.

Instead of following his example, practitioners seem more concerned with rank and unimportant organizational matters. Since there is no actual competition in Aikido, like in Judo for example, all sorts of people can operate in this environment. However, there seems to be a lot of competition on a political level, where some people can work safely in the shadows. This gives politicians an unchallenged chance to rise to the top and take control. Some great martial artists train in Aikido, but others lack technical skill; these people could not survive in another martial art. This is a paradox of the art. Only students who train hard and become technically proficient can concern themselves with spiritual and philosophical dimensions. Others who do not reach this level, or who do not want to make the sacrifices it requires, should not talk about peace and harmony and nonviolent conflict resolution, because they really do not understand these issues. O-Sensei talked about such matters, but only after training for decades to become one of the top fighters in Japan.

The way of nonviolence, or being a pacifist, is a choice one has to make from a powerful position. You are not a pacifist or peaceful person if you have no other choice. If you have to avoid a confrontation because you could not do anything about it, you are not a pacifist. If I could end a violent confrontation by injuring or killing my attacker, but I choose not to act violently and instead find a peaceful resolution to the conflict, then and only then am I a pacifist or a man of peace. Unfortunately, I think there are some people in Aikido and possibly other martial arts who pretend they are choosing the way of harmony but really could not do anything else. I began training in Judo in Germany, and the attraction that I had to martial arts at the time was because I wanted to be a stronger person, someone who could take care of himself. I did not want to be intimidated by an aggressive bully. I think that the attraction people have to most martial arts is the same today. By training hard, practitioners can become stronger. Their techniques can become martially effective. After enough training, if they ever find themselves in situations in which they have to defend themselves or protect others, they can be successful. If this was not the desire, then why would anyone train in martial arts?

Be careful about your own motives. There is nothing wrong with feeling vulnerable and trying to become strong, but do not lie to yourself and pretend that you are doing it for other more noble reasons. If you do this, you have become a martial arts actor, and you have left the real path. You are no longer training in Budo, and O-Sensei always upheld that Aikido is Budo. After decades of training, you will forget why you originally started on the path. You will train just for the sake of training. When this happens, the destination has become the path itself. This training then has a purity and sincerity to it, which is beautiful. It becomes a real part of your life, nothing else.

Choose your teachers by those same standards. Those who are famous with many followers are not necessarily the best. In fact, the great teachers in any field have always tried to avoid public fame and its pitfalls. A good teacher should have the qualities of a good *chawan* (tea bowl). The Japanese have a special word to describe the bittersweet taste of an unripe persimmon. This is called *shibui*, and its meaning goes far beyond "taste." Shibui is associated with an intimate understanding of the natural essence and simple beauty that exists at the heart of all classic Japanese arts. Those of us who train to transcend ourselves and sincerely practice Budo not only as a physical martial art, but also as a vehicle toward deeper (-spiritual) understanding, must become familiar with this concept. It helps us to become wiser, so that we are not moved or fooled by flamboyant and artificial people and things. We can use a great tea bowl to illustrate this quality.

75. Black Raku Tea Bowl

Tea ceremony utensils, and tea bowls in particular, are chosen for their ability to reflect the quality of shibui. The best have always been those whose feeling and look induce an atmosphere of calm serenity that will aid in self-isolation from the outside world's negative influences. Those tea bowl aesthetics can help us to define our own path. The qualities that give the bowl its shibui are the same qualities we seek in our teachers and ourselves. Those attributes are simplicity, implicitness, humility, tranquility, naturalness, normality, coarseness, strength, and emptiness. When we examine the objectives of the path we follow, we find that perfection can be measured by the same standards used to judge a precious tea bowl.

76. A Tea Bowl called Ochiba, which means "Falling Leaves."

The great martial arts teachers and Budo practitioners of the past led lives that reflected these same qualities. They were known by their simple yet exquisite ways. Shunning publicity, they preferred to be plain. They were implicit, stressing the inner meaning in themselves, as well as recognizing the "suchness" of all things in the universe. They were known for their modesty, never seeking credit or advancement despite their helpfulness to others. They preferred silence and tranquility, and they found them in a world where serenity is seemingly nonexistent. They leaned toward natural things, which made them spontaneous people who did not lead rote existences. They were content while moving about without affectation. At times, they were rough yet refined. They were not perfect. Just as some beautiful tea bowls have cracks and imperfections, Budo practitioners also were not perfect. (A related Japanese art form is called *kintsukuroi*. It is the art of piecing together broken pottery with gold or silver lacquer, thus realizing that the piece is more beautiful after breaking.) Finally, they were filled with that wondrous emptiness that enabled them to absorb their world with an awareness that invited others to follow the example they set. They were warriors because they had beaten themselves, and in doing so, had no need for further battles.

The observance or practice of any ritual without deep understanding of its aims is meaningless and without value. To practice martial arts in an effective way leads to qualities like tranquility, precision, courtesy, dignity, awareness, and selflessness. To gain these qualities, we should reflect upon the refined tea bowl, becoming shibui ourselves. This is the astringent taste of hard training, the nuance of restrained beauty in our art.

The Buddha, preaching silently among the rocks.

Sando, 1973.

77. The Buddha, preaching silently among rocks

CHAPTER 24:
UNDERLYING PRINCIPLES

*A*ikido quickly changed after O-Sensei died. It has continued to deteriorate. I did not want anything to do with Aikido politics; I just wanted to train the way that O-Sensei did, and I was unable to do so in Hawaii. Our art business there was successful, and I had made some money, so we decided to move to Montana, where I could train in Aikido away from politics. We bought a ranch that is located about fourteen miles outside of Kalispell, and we raised Arabian horses for many years. After getting settled, I opened a dojo. There was only one other dojo in Montana, and it was 120 miles away.

I visited a few dojo outside our state to introduce myself. Certainly, practitioners who follow the same path have a lot in common. I visited a Ki Society dojo in Spokane, Washington, which supposedly followed Tohei Sensei's teachings, but I was highly disappointed. I watched a class, but nothing they did resembled what Tohei Sensei taught. They did not use any of the same training exercises, and all the techniques seemed martially ineffective. Tohei Sensei was a strong martial artist. When Aikido was first introduced to the West, he was challenged by large men who were great fighters, and he held his own. He proved that Aikido is martially effective. However, nothing done in a dojo that claimed to follow his teachings resembled what he did at all. People were taking high break falls for no reason. At one point, the instructor asked the students to extend their energy into their partners, and they were falling to the ground once they supposedly felt the ki. I cannot believe how absurd the activity was. The people in the dojo did not know anything at all about internal energy or how to use it. They were pretending. Either that, or they really believed that they were correctly using an internal energy source. If this is the case, there was definitely some sort of brainwashing going on.

At one point, the instructor came over to speak to me, and I told him that I had once trained with Tohei, and that I had recently opened a dojo in Kalispell, which was about a five- or six-hour drive away. At the end of class, he asked his students to send some ki toward my new dojo. All of the students look to the East, and they did some unusual things with their facial features and body positions. I do not know what it was, but it had nothing to do with ki. I turned to him and said, "Thank you, Sensei, but I do not need your ki." If that is what has become of Tohei Sensei's Aikido, I am glad I left.

The following parable illustrates the type of brainwashing and misunderstandings that have permeated Aikido and some other modern martial arts, and it also demonstrates my unusual sense of humor:

The legendary Won Hong Lo was the founder of the No Kan Do style of Aikido. All new Aikido schools are in his direct lineage. He was so legendary that even the legends are legendary. One legend involves a senior student questioning him. "Oh, my learned teacher," the student said humbly, "what happened to all the ninja who once roamed the land?"

The old teacher smiled knowingly. He responded, "Do you not know that the ninja were masters of invisibility?"

The student had heard that they could vanish at will, and he knew that some people spent a lot of money to learn this skill. Usually, their teachers made their money disappear first. The teacher continued, "Yes, the ninja were not frauds. Their students were not wasting their time and money on worthless nonsense. The proof lies before our very eyes. All the ninja have simply vanished from our view. They are demonstrating by not showing themselves that they have mastered the art of invisibility."

The student was pleased with this answer. It made sense to him. He then asked another question: "What became of the secret teaching of the delayed death touch? Can this power be real?"

The instructor laughed. "Oh, what shall I do with you?" he said. "Of course there is a delayed death touch, and I am a master of it. It was passed on to me by the great master Fooyou, who was also legendary."

"You are?" the student exclaimed, his eyes opening widely.

"Yes, of course," the master responded. "Every man, woman, and child I have ever touched will eventually feel the results of this special technique. Their deaths may be soon or they might take years and years, but sooner or later, everyone I touch will die."

The student could not help but marvel at his master's wisdom.

Like the teacher in this parable, some martial arts instructors out there pretend that they have mastered secret techniques or that they possess some divine wisdom that they gained while meditating between television shows. Some may have even convinced themselves of such truths, as in some modern martial arts, like new-age Aikido, attackers do not fight back. They even attack in such a way that they are double-weighted and off balance, so they can be more easily thrown. Because of this, some instructors are able to get away with this type of fraud. And like the student in the parable, some students are seeking something hidden or deep within the martial arts, and they do not know where to look for it. Wanting desperately to find it, they latch on to some so-called successful instructor who has trophies and a lavishly decorated dojo, and they train. However, all of these people, students and teacher alike, misunderstand the true purpose of Budo. And if they train in Aikido, they should follow the founder. They should train the way he taught. Otherwise, why call the art Aikido?

I thought about Aikido's deterioration a lot, and I did not understand why people were practicing the way they were, why instructors who knew nothing were teaching things they themselves did not understand. Even today, it does not make sense to me, so I keep to myself, and I train in the art to the best of my capabilities, based upon what I was taught by my teachers, including O-Sensei, Tohei Koichi, and Takahashi Isao. This has given me a lot of time to practice and study, and I have come to realize that many people do not understand how traditional martial arts were structured, and this lack of understanding has perhaps resulted in individuals believing that such arts are synonymous with sports.

The actual structure of a ryu is complex and sophisticated by modern standards. Daito-ryu Aikijujutsu, the system from which Aikido was derived, was not originally a collection of empty hand techniques alone. The art also contained spear techniques from Hosoin-ryu, sword techniques from Ono-ha Itto-ryu, and of course, the empty-hand techniques of Takeda-ryu jujutsu. The empty-handed techniques were divided into categories: *ikkajo*, *nikka-jo*, *sankajo*, *yonkajo*, and *gokajo*. These in turn were divided into *nagewaza* (throwing techniques), *katamewaza* (pinning techniques), and *ate* (striking).

The interrelationship of these disciplines into a cohesive system is *riai*. It is not just a collection of techniques and tricks learned randomly. If you learn an attack like *yokomen* from Kendo, and a *koshinage* from Judo, you have two separate and unrelated techniques. A true ryu of the old Budo system had riai. The unique aspect of riai is that all techniques are the same in principle and are interchangeable. Each technique is a single and complete move, and it can be successfully performed both while empty-handed and with a variety of weapons. It does not matter if your opponent is armed or unarmed. The technique is always the same. In Aikido, it is often said that the way of the hand and the way of the sword is the same. This does not mean that the techniques look the same. It means, rather, that they are identical in all underlying aspects, especially the principles that are revealed in the techniques themselves. It has nothing to do with how the techniques look. In other words, the principle that makes them work is the same.

In many traditional martial arts, the underlying principles were never explicitly taught. It was the student's job to figure them out after years of training the external physical techniques. Confucius, when describing a good student, said that a teacher should show one corner. If the student did not then retire and figure out the remaining three corners for himself or herself, the teacher should refuse to instruct further. Perhaps this teaching has infused the Japanese martial arts, just as many other Chinese customs and philosophies have influenced Japanese culture. No matter where it came from, students who practice a traditional martial art must first learn how to learn. They must pay close attention to what their instructor is doing. Then they must duplicate the physical techniques. After years, they must begin to analyze the art's techniques objectively, seeking to understand the riai behind them.

We train in the basic techniques of Aikido until these principles are understood. By understanding, I mean a true and deep comprehension, not an intellectual or imagined idea of it. *Kihon suburi* are cutting exercises with a sword, which can help to develop *kokyu*. *Shikko*, or Japanese knee walking, helps to free up the hips, making it easier to move in all directions. The actual body movements used in Aikido, called *tai sabaki* or *tai no henka* is trained in each individual technique. If the physical techniques in this first stage are not understood, progress into the higher realms of the art is not possible. If students train diligently, however, they will eventually comprehend all the basic movements. They will understand the logic behind them. Once this occurs, the student will naturally progress to higher levels of study, including *aiki* and *kiai*.

O-Sensei said, "Aiki is the art of defeating your opponent with a single glance." This simple statement reflects the fundamental principle that exists in all things. It should not be mistaken for some magical or mysterious power. To understand aiki, we must understand kiai. The Sino-Japanese characters for both words are the same, only in reverse order. A literal translation of these kanji is "joining spirit" and "spirit joining," and they refer to the coming together of body, breath, and mind. When everything is working in perfect harmony, kiai exists. A sound is not always forthcoming, but such sounds are hard to suppress. Practitioners who train in an art that does not have kiai lack ability and understanding, because a comprehension of aiki is impossible without it. O-Sensei had a powerful kiai, and his students could feel it pierce their bodies. Proper kiai has this kind of feel. It cannot be rationally explained, but it is instantly recognized. It should send a shiver down your spine when you first hear or feel it. It will normally start before the technique reaches *kime* (focus of energy) and it may even end before this point. You could say that there is no kime without kiai. Its intensity should match the technique. When your techniques are good enough, kiai will naturally result. Do not force it or fake it. Forcing it is like forcing a technique; it does not work.

Aiki is the effect of kiai on your opponent. It is not the surprise or shock of a sudden scream like some beginners may think. Rather, it is being overcome by the focused and unified power of mind and spirit. Aiki is the linguistic opposite of kiai, and there are subtle differences in use and application. Aiki appears when you have reached a level of unshakable faith and confidence in your art, when there are no more doubts, and you no longer use force or fight. At this point, you are beyond life and death, ego, victory, and other desires. You are free of attachments. When an opponent faces someone like this, who has eliminated desires, in a real life and death situation, he or she can be defeated with a single glance.

Ki is a feeling of flow and universal correctness, which extends into your techniques. It is not a mysterious, immeasurable force. All Budo uses ki, but some arts train specifically to develop it. Good teachers emphasize it. Within the martial arts, there are two aspects, and the same traits really exist in all things. *Ji* refers to techniques. *Ri* is a term used to describe principles behind them. A person who fully understands the underlying principles has no difficulties in the performance of various techniques.

Practice should entail studying the underlying principles. Budo practitioners are independent students, not members, clients, patients, or followers. The emphasis is on learning, being open to learn about ourselves and, as Dogen reminds us, ultimately about "the whole thing." No one can discover those principles for you. You cannot buy them and you cannot fake them, for a person who understands aiki will see right through you. You have to do it for yourself! This is what Budo teaches: self-reliance and wisdom. Without austere and sincere training, no one will ever become proficient. This understanding applies to all things. Stupidity is changeable by training, and it is impossible to become a master without transforming stupidity. When you train in one art thoroughly and honestly, it becomes possible to master that art. All human beings, in one respect or another, are ignorant. Disciplined training can help to eliminate this ignorance. After enough training, principles are understood and wisdom appears. To study the way is to study the self. To study the self is to forget the self. To forget the self is to be enlightened by all things, and to understand the fundamental principle of the universe.

Journeys on Mind Mountain.

78. Journeys on Mind Mountain

CHAPTER 25:
THE TEA CEREMONY AND ITS MARTIAL CONNECTION

79. Tea Ceremony by artist Mizuno Toshikata (1866 – 1908)

I have spent decades studying what O-Sensei and my other teachers taught. I have also continued to train in calligraphy and art, and I collect swords, artwork, and tea bowls. I am particularly fond of tea bowls, and am interested in the tea ceremony, which has always been associated with the martial arts. Some students will not understand why this is so. They should not be embarrassed, as some famous warriors also did not originally understand the connection. Toyotomi Hideyoshi was the most powerful samurai in the country. In his free time, he studied the tea ceremony, learning how to serve tea. He was taught by the famous Sen no Rikyu. One of Toyotomi's generals thought that he was spending too much time learning a servant's art, and did not understand why a shogun would ever need to serve tea to guests. Since his lord would not stop training, the vassal decided to kill the tea master. He attended a tea ceremony, intending to strike him down as soon as he detected an opening. However, Sen no Rikyu maintained zanshin the entire time. He was completely concentrated on the task, yet displayed a complete awareness of everything that was occurring around him. Toyotomi's vassal then understood why his master studied under this man. The Way of Tea was the same as the Way of the Samurai, and his martial awareness was honed in the teahouse.

Another legend involves the samurai daimyo Yamanouchi and his tea master. At the end of the seventeenth century, Lord Yamanouchi of Tosa Province had to make an official trip to Edo. This was due to a policy put into place by the Tokugawa Shogunate, which required all retainers to spend every third year in the capital. He wanted to bring his tea master with him, but the master was nervous. He had heard stories about the rough individuals in Edo, and he was not a fighter. The daimyo was insistent, and eventually the master had to give in. He put away his normal kimono, and attired as a samurai vassal, accompanied his lord to the capital. He wore two swords, as was customary. For the most part, he spent his days in the lord's private residence, but since this was his first time outside of Tosa, he wanted to do some sightseeing. Having obtained permission to do so, he walked around the Shinobazu pond in the Ueno district. There he came upon a mean-looking ronin.

At first, he thought of turning around and finding another way, but he did not think that this would be a solution to his problem, as the warrior would likely get up and follow him. He decided to walk right past him, and as he passed, the man turned to him and said, "I can see that you are a samurai vassal of Tosa. It would be a great honor to practice my swordsmanship with you." This was a direct challenge. Since the tea master had no skill whatsoever with the sword, his mind went crazy trying to find excuses, a way out of this bout. Eventually, he told the truth. He explained that even though he appeared to be a samurai, he was nothing more than a student of the Way of Tea. He performed the tea ceremony for his lord.

In truth, the ronin did not care about practicing his swordsmanship; he did not really want to duel. Instead, he wanted to take the passerby's money. Now that he knew his potential victim could not defend himself, he wanted to have a match even more. He planned to slay him and then rob him. The tea master found no way out of the situation, and he was determined to die a noble death, which would reflect highly upon Tosa. The problem was that he did not know how to die an honorable death as a samurai. On his way to the park, he had passed a swordsmanship school. The tea master then thought that if he could postpone the bout, he could return to the school and ask the master there to teach him how to die properly. He told the ronin, "I will have a match with you, but I am busy on an errand for my master. Once I have completed this, I will return."

The ronin consented, and the tea master went directly to the sword school and appeared before the instructor. He explained to him what had happened, and he asked him how to die properly. The sword master said, "Students who come to train with me generally want to know how to use a sword, so that they do not die. This is the first case in which a student has come to me asking how to die. I will teach you how to die in a manner befitting of a samurai, but first, please make tea for me."

"I am honored to do so," the tea master said, and he got ready for the ceremony. The sword instructor knelt on tatami and watched the preparation. The tea master seemingly had no thought whatsoever about his impending death. He was completely focused on the task, making tea, and every move was deliberate. He maintained complete mindfulness, and treated the act as though it were the most important thing in the world.

At the end of the ceremony, the sword master said, "There is no need for you to learn how to die. I am certain that you will die well. Your state of mind when you are performing the tea ceremony is exactly the same state of mind that one strives to cultivate in the art of the sword. When you see the ronin, think of him as a guest in your teahouse. Be courteous and apologize for the lateness of your arrival. Tell him that you are ready to face him in combat. Remove your haori, fold it, and then place your fan on top of it in the same manner as you do before you serve tea. Then, place a *tenugui* around your head, tie up the sleeves of your kimono, so they do not get in the way, and pull up your hakama, so that you do not trip over it. After having completed these preparations, you are ready to begin. Draw your sword and raise it into striking position. In this position, collect your thoughts, breathe deeply and prepare. When you hear your opponent yell, cut straight down with your sword as quickly and decisively as possible. The match will likely end in *aiuchi*, mutual killing. This is an honorable death."

The tea master went back to the ronin. He followed the sword teacher's instructions. He raised his sword into *jodan*, a position in which the blade is directly over his head, and then he glared at his opponent. The ronin did not see the same weak tea master as before. Instead, he saw fearless warrior, a man who did not fear death. He did not see a single opening in the tea master's defenses, so there was nowhere he could safely strike without being struck himself. He quickly backed up and then drop to the ground, prostrate. He bowed, apologizing for his rude request, and begged to be spared. The tea master lowered his sword, and the ronin left the scene as quickly as possible.[53]

These tales might just be legends, but they have been told for hundreds of years and passed down to the present to teach a lesson. A profound and explicit connection exists between martial disciplines and Zen-related arts, such as the tea ceremony. Teaism is sometimes thought of as a cult, as it is much more than drinking tea. It is the adoration of beautiful things among the sordid elements of the outside world. It is the admiration of simplicity. The tearoom (*sukiya*) is a small building that appears like a cottage or straw hut. The original characters for sukiya meant "the abode of the fancy," but the modern Japanese term for it means "the abode of emptiness" or "the abode of the unsymmetrical." The structure itself praises emptiness. Daoist ideals are reflected in Zen, as the former influenced the later before its introduction to Japan. The Dao De Ching contains the following teaching:

> *Thirty spokes will converge in the hub of a wheel; but the use of the cart will depend on the part of the hub that is void. With the wall all around, a clay bowl is molded; but the use of the bowl will depend on the part of the bowl that is void. Cut out windows and doors in the house as you build; but the use of the house will depend on the space in the walls that is void. So advantage is had from whatever is there; but usefulness rises from whatever is not.*[54]

Okakura Kakuzo explained the design of the tearoom:

> *It is an abode of fancy inasmuch as it is an ephemeral structure built to house a poetic impulse. It is an abode of vacancy*

inasmuch as it is devoid of ornamentation except for what may be placed in it to satisfy some aesthetic need of the moment. It is an abode of the unsymmetrical inasmuch as it is consecrated to the worship of the imperfect, purposely leaving something unfinished for the play of the imagination to complete.[55]

This understanding of the importance of emptiness is also found in martial arts. If one is truly empty (of all thoughts and vacillations) he can dominate any situation. "One who could make himself a vacuum into which others might freely enter would become master of all situations. The whole can always dominate the part."[56] Some common fixtures in martial arts dojo are also attributed to the tearoom, like the *tokonoma*. Tearooms used tokonoma, and they were decorated with folding screens, scrolls displaying calligraphy or paintings, and artistically arranged flowers – an art form called ikebana.

The tea ceremony is difficult for outsiders to understand. The ceremony itself has certain rules of etiquette called *sarei*. People who have never been to the cha no yu might wonder why it matters how a person drinks tea, or why it matters how it was prepared. If it tastes the same, what could possibly be the difference? This might be because people drink tea every day, and the actual drinking is certainly not considered an art form. Once it is done in a tearoom, and the tea is prepared in a ritualistic manner, the guests adhering to certain rules, it becomes a thing of beauty. It is no longer mundane, but an art form that celebrates the beauty in day-to-day life.

The powdered green tea used in the tea ceremony was introduced from (Sung) China in the early Kamakura period (at the end of the twelfth century) by Eisai, and in time, it became influenced by Zen. Today, there is a Japanese expression *chazen ichimi*, which means "tea and zen have the same flavor." In addition, the popular expression *ichi go ichi e* (one time, one meeting) supposedly originated with the cha no yu. It signifies that each moment of life is unique and special, and it will not occur again. Therefore, one must live in the present, so he or she can fully appreciate it.

Another aesthetic is also found in tea ceremony utensils: wabi. The cha no yu became popular in feudal Japan among samurai and townspeople alike. A study of the utensils used included a sentiment called wamono, an appreciation of plainness and unpolished beauty. Yasuhiko explained this:

The noun wabi derives from wabu (to be wretched) or wabishii (wretched) and originally referred to the miserable feeling that comes from material deprivation. Wabi became a meaningful aesthetic term in the world of waka poetry at the end of the ancient age and the beginning of medieval times, when Saigyo and other inja emerged and voluntarily pursued lives of loneliness and deprivation, forcing themselves to deal with wabishii living conditions. Fujiwara no Shunzei and his son Teika also played significant roles in the development of the aesthetic of wabi at this time. Thus we see that wabi was not just associated with the chanoyu, but was used in the realm of poetry as a term related to sabi (loneliness). Wabi was taken into the world of chanoyu and made its aesthetic because, at the height of the craze for mono-suki (the taste for material things), chanoyu encountered wabi as an aesthetic based on things. Wabi was, indeed, the final point in the development of mono-suki. Yet we have noted that wabi originally implied a lack of things. The point, however, is not to be completely bereft of material possessions (since there would then be no need for an aesthetic): wabi does not mean to deny things, but rather to penetrate as far as possible to their true essence and therein to discern beauty. In the beauty of the plain lies the ultimate sense of beauty that the Japanese have discovered. Wabi goes beyond the aesthetics of things and becomes a state of mind.[57]

80. Another tea bowl demonstrating shibui and wabi.

This state of mind is sought in the martial arts, and this is one of the reasons why the two paths are not separate. It is why accomplished warriors also trained in the Art of Tea. Another aesthetic found in tea ceremony utensils is *shibumi*, which means "astringency."

Shibumi is an elusive aspect of Japanese aestheticism. The adjective, which has been previously described, is shibui. It is derived from *shibu*: low-keyed, simple, unaffected, tasty, and elegant. However, like many Japanese expressions, there is no direct translation for this term, and the definitions for it do not accurately reflect its meaning. Like all transcendent qualities, the word shibumi eludes defining. To the Japanese, external things that soothe and satisfy the spirit are shibumi. These things are instinctive, not shaped by reason and not easily put into words, but the term suggests art appreciation, culture, refinement, quiet tastes, and a consideration for others. The idea of "nothing too much" is in it, and the word protests ostentation. It conveys a quality that confirms the traditional appreciation of serenity, introspection, modesty, formality, nobility, and reserve. It is opposed to everything that is garish, lewd, sensuous, or noisy.

No single English word exactly describes shibumi as it is understood by the Japanese. I think the following is a good translation of it: "the epitome of elegance and refinement: the result of the use of restraint in the highest sense." The Japanese speak of shibui in relation to customs, houses, rooms, decorations, people, dress, as well as tone of voice. It marks the character of the old order of things, sometimes also of the new. In short, the parts must be related to the whole, and the whole must accord with place and circumstance. Shibumi is found in all Japanese arts – that esoteric quality introduced into art by Zen Buddhism. It is the art that conceals art.

A certain color scheme is essential in producing a shibumi effect. A sculptured piece of white marble, for instance, cannot be shibui because it is devoid of color, but the prevalence of brilliant white is antagonistic to shibui. The color of bran, the outer coat of rice and wheat kernels, is commonly called *shibui-kawa*, (which literally means astringent skin). This color, or various shades of chestnut or russet, is usually essential in securing a shibui effect. The color of ashes, unpolished silver and gold, and other similar colors can produce a subdued and tranquil effect. The artistic employment of such colors and combinations of colors imparts an indescribable shibumi. A careful study of Japanese houses' guest rooms reveals that the color scheme is obtained by the contrast of the colors of the walls, ceilings, pillars, and other parts of the room. In no part of it is there a gaudy or bright color which would depart from the traditional colors used to create shibumi.

Commenting on a woman's kimono, a Japanese person might say, "Look at her shibui konomi," which means that the woman is dressed in a kimono that is not flashy, but made with subdued colors. Despite its humble appearance, however, it is rich in quality. In speaking of voice as shibui, reference is made to its quality due to cultivation and training. Perhaps a literal rendition of the meaning of shibui konomi is "an inherent appreciation of the elements, properly arranged and balanced, which are found centered in art, and in one's life and personality." This same quality is sought in the martial arts.

**81. At the ancient pond
a frog jumps in
the sound of water.
Basho Matsuo (1644–1694)**

CHAPTER 26:
SEN NO RIKYU

82. Tea house in Okayama, Japan

*S*en no Rikyu (1522-1591) is the most famous tea master. Born in Sakai, Izumi Province, his family was wealthy and like others in the area, they sold fish. Sakai at the time was a hotspot for poets, painters, Zen priests, and entertainers. It was a cultural center that rivaled Kyoto. The tea ceremony was popular in Sakai, but it was an emerging art form. Sen no Rikyu was drawn to it. In his twenties, he took the Buddhist name Soeki and mastered it. Later in life, he went by the name Rikyu Koji. He changed certain elements of the ceremony. Rather than use expensive items, as others in Sakai were prone to do, he chose items that had a sense of wabi: simple yet refined implements. He also changed the entranceway. He made it small – so small, in fact, that one had to crawl to enter. It was only sixty-six square centimeters, and it was called *nijiriguchi*, "crawling-in entrance."

I remember entering O-Sensei's office at the old dojo, and the door was so small that I had to crawl in on my hands and knees. The prevalence of such small doors in Japanese culture might have stemmed from Sen no Rikyu's addition of this pre-existing cultural phenomenon to the tea ceremony. Supposedly, he modeled this doorway after the small entryway through which one had to pass to enter a boat's cabin. While he was on a riverboat at Hirakata in Osaka, he used such a small hatch, and he thought that it had a wabi feeling. After this, he introduced it to the teahouse. However, there is more to it than this. People who enter ships step foot into another realm that is separate from the outside world. The doorway, as it is used in teahouses, also finds a predecessor in the theater entranceways. They were small openings, and people had to crawl inside. The idea behind this was to separate the outside world from the fantasy realm that the ticket holders were entering. "The entranceways to theaters that we see pictured in paintings of the period were exceedingly small apertures, appropriately named "mouse wickets," that resembled nijiriguchi. By crawling through the mouse wicket, people entered a world of the theater separate from the everyday space in which they usually moved. They entered, indeed, a world of dramatic space."[58]

Passing through a small space to enter another world was also associated with the Shugendo religion, which was popular in Sakai. Believers spent their days performing austerities in the mountains. They engaged in grueling, torturous practices, such as meditating under waterfalls, performing cold-water ablutions, and cutting out all grains for three thousand days at a time. Some of them even took action to mummify themselves, and some bodies are today displayed at Kaiko Temple, in Sakata.[59] Many Shugendo practitioners, called *shugenja*, were also known as fearsome warriors, and they were often equated with tengu, the mythical bird-like creatures who supposedly taught sword techniques to many of the most famous warriors in Japanese history. The shugenja had a practice called *tainai kuguri*, which literally means, "to pass through the womb." They crawled through small holes among rocks on mountainsides as part of a spiritual quest. When they emerged, they had been symbolically reborn. Such men also meditated in mountain caves and they entered dangerous, small openings on cliff sides, just to meditate and fast within the caves. After several days, they would emerge from the tiny aperture and greet the world as newborn, more spiritual beings. Keeping in mind the inseparability of Japanese traditions like the tea ceremony, theater and Shugendo, and the use of tiny doors in each of them, it can be surmised that such portals serve two functions:

1. They serve as a symbolic entrance to another sacred world, a different dimension.

2. They symbolize the womb, which indicates that those who enter can be reborn. They can emerge as different people.

The tearoom, in this sense, is a sacred place, just like the revered mountain caves in which shugenja meditated. The dojo, too, should be thought of as a sacred place. The reason shoes are removed stems from the early Japanese custom of visitors removing their shoes upon entering a temple, a holy location.

We enter a traditional dojo opposite the **kamiza** at the **shimosa**. Our intellect, our conscious desire to learn brings us to the entrance. This is the first barrier. This is where we must leave our intellect. Beginners who appear at the shimosa full of preconceptions are unlikely to progress unless they leave their opinions and ideas behind and offer themselves empty to the art's teachings. At first, beginners will describe their experiences as cerebral, even if they try to set their preconceptions aside. They stumble and are lost, unable to do anything instinctively or in an intuitive manner.

At the shimosa, novices learn dojo manners, which permit them to conduct themselves in a dignified manner, to practice safely in a hazardous atmosphere, and to develop consideration for others. Respect and manners must begin at the entrance and continue into the outside world after leaving the dojo. The joseki is at the right of the kamiza and symbolizes virtue and charity. It is the place occupied by teachers and the senior students when they initially line up and during practice. Although many do not stop to consider such things, this area of the dojo should remind us all that the future of traditional martial arts depends on successive generations. The senior students have the honor of caring for the lower ranks and bringing them forward. This is their responsibility.

The shomen (front) is where the kamiza is located. It is the dojo's spiritual center. The tokonoma is an alcove or shrine in the kamiza, where a picture of the founder and a scroll is located. It is generally rather bare, like a tearoom, and it should reflect a sense of wabi. The kamiza, in its entirety, should elevate the importance of what goes on in the dojo in front of it, and it should direct students to the spiritual aspects of the art. The *shimoseki* side of the dojo (opposite the shimosa) is where new students concentrate their activities. The principal quality they must have is a sense of moral appropriateness of what they are doing. They must know that their seniors wish only the best for them, and that their seniors expect them to do their best. In this way, they can achieve their goals. For this reason, morality and integrity are the dominant components of the shimoseki.

Is one side, the joseki or the shimoseki, more important than the other? I do not think so. The joseki is always examined consciously and subconsciously by the kohai. Juniors watch and evaluate their sempai. Are the sempai's actions and lifestyle in accordance with their teaching and highest ideals of the art? Do the seniors demand more of new students than they can or are willing to do? The shimoseki, with its emphasis on integrity, is the perfect location in which to spot hypocrisy or pretentiousness on the other side, the joseki. Wise novices use it in this way: a vantage point from which they can evaluate the ideals of the art and their sempai.

The embujo is the dojo's center, the place where all trainees meet. This is where conflict is initiated and then resolved. Here rationalization, however clever and well reasoned, is insufficient. At the center, students must do their best and make no excuses. While this sounds easy in an abstract manner, it is difficult to put into practice, as the temptation to protect one's ego is almost overwhelming. Protecting the sense of ego, students resort to all kinds of explanations and excuses, silently and aloud to others. However, at the heart of the dojo, all are superfluous. All that matters is what is done or what is not done. No excuse or explanation is needed. Nor could it make any difference.

The dojo truly is a spiritual place, and the entrance to the dojo serves to separate it from the outside world, just as a *torii* gate separates a Shinto shrine from the secular realm. However, the entrance must eventually cease to serve as a boundary. The outside world and the dojo must become one. This does not mean that the training space is no longer considered sacred and important. It is just the opposite. The sense of reverence that one develops in the dojo must transcend the location. It must be applied to the world at large.

When this happens, training stops being something special. It becomes ordinary, yet it turns out to be a necessary part of life.

Omori Sogen explained that Zen can manifest in everyday activities, such as cutting vegetables, sewing, and keeping accounts, never mind art forms typically associated with Zen, like calligraphy and the tea ceremony. He pointed out that it is important not to "limit their discipline to the time of their particular practice. What is practiced and learned while doing calligraphy or picking tea leaves should be joined with the rest of one's life."[60] Peaceful arts can help practitioners to discover themselves. If this is the case, imagine how much more effective activities in which one faces life and death can be. Mann wrote, "If such mundane activities hold the potential to shed light on the true nature of human existence, how much more so those activities in which one is forced to stare mortality square in the face?"[61]

This confrontation with life and death was experienced firsthand by the famed tea master Sen no Rikyu. (There are many tales told about why Hideyoshi ordered him to commit suicide. No one knows for sure. The following is one version.) He was accused of being implicated in a plot to poison Lord Hideyoshi, and some of his enemies spread the rumor that the lord was going to be served a cup of tea that contained the lethal dose. Even if this rumor was not true, the tea master's death was ordered. Rikyu was permitted one privilege only: he could take his own life by disemboweling himself, as was the samurai custom of the time. On the day of his death, he invited his disciples and friends to attend one final tea ceremony. Okakura Kakuzo explained what occurred:

Mournfully at the appointed time the guests meet at the portico. As they look into the garden path the trees seem to shudder, and in the rustling of their leaves are heard the whispers of homeless ghosts. Like solemn sentinels before the gates of Hades stand the grey stone lanterns. A wave of rare incense is wafted from the tea room; it is the summons which bids the guests to enter. One by one they advance and take their places. In the tokonoma hangs a kakemono, a wonderful writing by an ancient monk dealing with the evanescence of all earthly things.

The singing kettle, as it boils over the brazier, sounds like some cicada pouring forth his woes to departing summer. Soon the host enters the room. Each in turn is served with tea, and each in turn silently drains his cup, the host last of all. According to established etiquette, the chief guest now asks permission to examine the tea equipage. Rikyu places the various articles before them, with the kakemono. After all have expressed admiration of their beauty, Rikyu presents one of them to each of the assembled company as a souvenir. The bowl alone he keeps. "Never again shall this cup, polluted by the lips of misfortune, be used by man." He speaks, and breaks the vessel into fragments.

The ceremony is over; the guests, with difficulty restraining their tears, take their last farewell and leave the room. One only, the nearest and dearest, is requested to remain and witness the end. Rikyu then removes his tea gown and carefully folds it upon the mat, thereby disclosing the immaculate white death robe which it had hitherto concealed. Tenderly he gazes on the shining blade of the fatal dagger, and in exquisite verse thus addresses it:

Welcome to thee,
O sword of eternity!
Through Buddha
And through the Dharuma alike
Thou hast cleft thy way.

With a smile on his face, Rikyu passes forth into the unknown.[62]

83. Gakuji Myogo Jizo-san: Respect to the Bodhisattva Jizo

CHAPTER 27:
DEVOTING ONE'S LIFE TO TRAINING

*L*ately, much has been written about O-Sensei and his connection to Aikido and farming. Because of this association, my wife and I left Honolulu many years ago, came to Montana, and bought land to start a ranch. At that time, good land was still available. We were fortunate to acquire a place with a beautiful view, rolling hills with good pasture, and a beautiful forest with a stream running through it. We started by building our own road. We built over two miles of fence, and we drilled a well for our water. The goal was to raise and breed Arabian horses, create an Aikido setting and be as self-sufficient as possible. This was a dream, and we were convinced we could make it into a reality.

The question I was asked the most was, "Do you think you can make a living?" I have thought about this and realized that one does not make a living; one simply lives a life. The definition of a conventional financial statement is narrow and leaves out the creation of value and the quality of one's life. By widening this definition, we can include factors that do not fit into the lines and boxes of a conventional financial statement. Our balance sheet looks good because the value of our ranch has appreciated considerably, and because we had built our house, stables, hay barns, and outbuildings with our own hands as money became available. Therefore, we have never been burdened with a mortgage and high interest rates. The occasional good year made up for a few bad years, and some investments, art, and other skills have enabled us to keep going. Consequently, our debts are reasonable in relation to our assets.

There is also the fact that we grow and provide food for friends and ourselves that is healthier than food bought in the supermarket. The labor we perform is not an expense but a product. It is healthy in itself, which means that we place no great burden on the healthcare system, as we would working more lucrative occupations in polluted and crime-ridden cities. Through our ranch and animals, we are able to live out our passion for this land. We are able to shape, nourish, and maintain our own surroundings according to our plans, which are frequently corrected and changed by nature, as opposed to our idea of what nature is all about. Slowly, step by step, season by season, one comes closer to the center of things as they really are, instead of how we think they are. You cannot get this from spending a couple of hours in a park.

The wealth that comes from the land is considerable, regardless how under-valued it is in the marketplace. Each year when the geese fly south and the days are getting shorter, I question myself: "Would I rather have money in a substantial savings account, a health plan, a pension plan, life insurance, yet hate the life I lead in order to have all those things?" We have chosen to live a life, not to endure one. The winter is near and the numbers are always unsat-isfactory, but even the winter with all its hardships is beautiful, and next year will always be better, without drought, flood, or hail or snow too late or too early. Next year I will be stronger, wiser, perhaps less idealistic, perhaps less of a dreamer. But the cycle will always be flawed. There can be no perfection, only dreams of it: dreams of the easy life and completion.

This dream is a labor of self-creation but also a self-defense against the commercial pressures of our time whose boundless resources are so artfully beamed into our minds and other spaces we think of as our own, and which will harness our needs, desires, fears, and fantasies to their own profitable ends. They shrink from no means to gain power over your imagination. Thus to dream a place, build it and work the land is an act of independence and even defiance against the mass-marketed artificial world.

However, the dream will fail. There is no perfection. There will be droughts, frosts and storms, but you can feel those things first hand. You can feel alive, and with your imagination and labor, you can overcome them. Creation and recreation! In a world of consumerism, instant gratification and artificial val-ues, this imagination and unification with the land are our most powerful and most human defense.

I have continued to train in Aikido, and to practice both calligraphy and Sumi-e, and I continue to collect artwork and historical pieces. The following poem sums up my sentiments:

It has come to this –

My love of art, my love of nature, is one.

I comfort in wilderness as others do in prayer.

Rocks and trees, rain and earth, cold and snow,

Stillness and solitude all nourish my body and soul.

God, nature, and I walk hand in hand.

Together we walk in wilderness –

Yet footprints in the snow show but one;

The wonder, the mystery.

It has come to this for me.

Life in Montana can be difficult, especially during the winter. The following is a well-known haiku: "Before enlightenment, chopping wood and carrying water. After enlightenment, chopping wood and carrying water." Some might use this statement to teach others about Zen, without actually living in this way, but this is what we did for decades. Every day, we had to take care of the horses and work the land. We carried water from the well and chopped wood. There was never an end to it. I also continued to teach at the dojo, and there have been many unique students who have shown up to practice, many of whom refused to "empty their cups," or who believed that they had some great understanding of an art they had only recently begun. This attitude will impede students' progress. Training should be to foster self-improvement, and to accomplish this aim, one must train in an effective manner. How dojo are run will help to guide new students along the correct path. Dojo hierarchy should be kept simple. The relationship between the teacher and the student is, in most cases, adequate. Seniors (sempai) are there to set an example by doing extra service assisting juniors (kohai) to learn, not to push people around. Self-deception is dangerous.

The ideals of Aikido should be put into practice in daily life, and they should be practical. If you talk a lot about ki energy, protecting life and changing the world, but do nothing to contribute to it, you are a fool and a hypocrite.

If you think you are understanding and doing those things, but instead are doing senseless, ridiculous, and useless things, you are dangerous. Ask yourself, "What are my true motives for training?" What do you plan to do with the skills and understanding gained from this training? You should gain an opportunity to help others and serve in an ordinary, mostly unseen, and egoless manner. Students who stay and train hard transform their lives and the lives of those around them. They should become peaceful warriors: free and outspoken citizens of the world. They should enhance their skills and go on to careers that nurture and protect society, dysfunctional as it is. They should be people of integrity, possessing the quality of a good tea bowl, shibui. Do not think O-Sensei's dream of a better world where all humans are one family is just going to happen because you showed up at the dojo a couple times a month when you felt like it. The secret of Budo training is a four-letter word: W-O-R-K. A Japanese expression, gambaru, means to do one's best, to work hard, and to persevere. It is commonly heard in the Japanese martial arts. Teachers say "gambatte" to their students, reminding them to continue to train hard, no matter what the setbacks might be. Just keep training.

Until you gain great skill and understanding of the heavenly principles underlying the physical techniques, you are a student. If you are afraid of life as it is, face it, change it, and be honest about it. Train hard, correctly and sincerely, so that you can get on to actually serving humanity. It can be done! Unless you drop out forever, it can be done. The aiki attitude and its potential for unconditional awakening is slowly infiltrating our world and working its transformative magic. There is no turning back. Anyone can participate, although not everyone can be a true teacher. Train, gain a more real perspective, and simply live a life of authentic integrity, growing where you need to grow, observing yourself, questioning your real motives, and noting how you improve without pride and too much ego. Do not have high expectations, just be the best you can be each day, one day at a time. Notice, discern, and respond as harmoniously as possible with strength and integrity.

When conflicts happen, it indicates that many small battles and opportunities were not addressed honestly. These then accumulate and turn into a dark large cloud of error, which inevitably explodes into a senseless madness in which many more errors are made. Complacency and neglect are dangerous. Quietly heroic actions and miracles happen every day, for the most part unrecognized. The fortitude to choose right action, harmonious action, separates the warrior from the coward. It is enough if each person responds to life's challenges with honesty, courage, resolve, purpose, and clarity as they arise. The voice of the inner observer, your true master, is clear. Everyone knows right from wrong. If you do not have this inner observer, you are not fully human. Training in the dojo will help you to foster such spiritual awareness. Life is not a contest. It is a cooperative endeavor. Look around you. This is not a rehearsal. This is it. Realize this, work honestly and diligently, and you will be successful.

84. Two Samurai Fighting

CHAPTER 28:
THE MOUNTAIN PATH

*T*he only thing that one must do to be successful in the martial arts, or in anything for that matter, is to never give up. Just show up and train. Ego and desire alone get in the way and prevent students from becoming their best. They might not want to lose, so they do not allow themselves to be put into weak positions. They might believe that they are skilled because of their previous experiences in other martial arts or even in seemingly unrelated fields. Individuals who have not learned to empty their cups will be relatively unsuccessful. The historical Buddha explained that suffering stems from desire; the only way to end suffering is to eliminate desire. Quit all desires. Just train. When students begin practicing a martial art, they have a white belt. In time, their blood and sweat turn the white to gray. After years, the gray darkens, until it eventually turns black. Having never considered themselves to have mastered anything, they do not stop. They just continue to practice and improve, always seeking the truth. After years pass, the black belt begins to fray, displaying various shades of gray. Eventually, it returns to white. This cycle can be demonstrated by the Zen enso.

Students begin on one end, learning basic techniques and stances. As they progress around the circle, they attain greater insights. About halfway through, at the top of the circle as it is typically displayed on scrolls, others consider them masters. They might believe that they are good too, but as they continue, they realize how little they actually know. Maintaining this view, they become open to receiving information, and their progress increases exponentially. They attain a beginner's mind and transcend perceived reality. Eventually, their training brings them to the end of the circle, which is just the beginning. They have a beginner's mind, even though they have truly mastered the art. Many parables in the martial arts attempt to explain the same thing, such as the overflowing teacup and the Zen circle. Others refer to Budo training in general. I think a mountain path is also an apt analogy.

Ueda Akinari (1734–1809) wrote a short story called *Shiramine* (*White Peak*), which was published in his collection *Ugetsu Monogatari* (*Tales of Moonlight and Rain*). The protagonist heads up a mountain in Matsuyama to visit the grave of the abdicated emperor. In the original Japanese, no subject pronouns are used in the narrative. The uninformed reader will not know who the characters are. But readers who have some knowledge about Japanese history will recognize the protagonist as the famous monk Saigyo (1118-1190), who wrote many well-known poems. The grave that he visits belongs to the exiled emperor Sutoku (1119-1164). In the tale, he heads up the mountain, until the pine and cypress trees grow so thickly together that nothing other than the mountain path can be seen. In addition, the mountain is covered with clouds, and a thick mist rises up from the valley. Everything is blanketed in white and gray. When he arrives at the grave, he encounters the ghost of the abdicated emperor, with whom he speaks at length. The ghost had taken up the practices of the tengu, and he claims responsibility for some misfortunate events that had historically occurred. The tale blends history and the supernatural, and it demonstrates that mountains are liminal places: between the worlds of the living and the dead. This sentiment has not dissipated in modern Japanese thinking. In Shinto, it is believed that mountains are the resting place of ancestral spirits, and a burial procession is still called *yamayuki*, which literally means "going to the mountain." This connection between life and death is clearly seen on some mountains in Japan, one of the most famous being Osorezan, in Aomori Prefecture.

85. Statue of Jizo Bosatsu, hidden in the gray fog at Osorezan. (Aomori, Japan).

Osorezan is an active volcano, and pockets of gas escape from the ground upon which visitors walk. It smells of sulfur, and if visitors are not careful, they can burn their hands on some of the rock formations there. Many rocks are piled together, and one can see toys and clothes strewn about on the ground. These are grave markers that relatives built to honor their deceased family members. The site is completely gray. The ground and stones are gray, and it is often covered in fog. *Miko,* Japanese shaman, come to the site several times yearly to invoke the presence of the deceased. It is truly a liminal place in which life and death are inexorably joined. If visitors wandered out into the fog without knowing where they were going, they might get lost, but eventually, they would come across some statues of Bodhisattvas, especially Jizo, the protector of lost travelers. Jizo is a guide, but his effigies can only be found by wandering into the grayness.

Mountains are a place in which the living and the dead are joined. In a sense, the same relationship is found in dojo. Practitioners learn how to kill, and they learn how to protect themselves. Eventually, they learn how to protect others. Then, this training leads to higher spiritual levels. When students begin training, they head up some path toward the summit, but they cannot yet see the summit. They also cannot see where the path upon which they traverse ends. Some end at different heights up the mountain, well short of the summit. Some practitioners might become enamored with the art's physical techniques, and they believe that perfecting such motions is all there is. Once this perfection happens, they find themselves at the end of their path, and they believe that they have mastered it – that they have reached the summit. But they are on a dead-end path. Others might train to understand internal energy and find themselves higher up the mountain, but when they think they have reached the summit, it is really just another dead end. There are many dead ends, and after training for long enough, some might begin to think that reaching the top is impossible. Therefore, when they look at people like O-Sensei, they think of him as superhuman, as he reached a summit that many others are unable to reach. Some are unable to find the correct path that leads there.

Many people like to view martial art masters of the past as more than human. They put them on pedestals and regard them as saint like. I think this is a mistake. Such individuals were remarkable people, but they were human, and it is foolish to think that you cannot reach their level. If you train hard enough, there are no limits to what you can attain. *Hagakure* contains the following admonition:

> *It is spiritless to think that you cannot attain to that which you have seen and heard the masters attain. The masters are men. You are also a man. If you think that you will be inferior in doing something, you will be on that road very soon. Master Ittei said, "Confucius was a sage because he had the will to become a scholar when he was fifteen years old. He was not a sage because he studied later on." This is the same as the Buddhist maxim, "First intention, then enlightenment."[63]*

My teacher, Takahashi Sensei, said, "If you want a hill, you must strive for a mountain," and Tohei Sensei used to describe people as ships on undulating ocean waves. They move around aimlessly, without direction, getting pushed and pulled this way and that way. He used to say that they should set their sights on a star. They will certainly never reach it, but they will become steady. They will have direction. Fix your sights on greatness, and follow the path toward it! Ueshiba Morihei O-Sensei was a remarkable martial artist, although he was an eccentric and old-fashioned person. Some people like to talk about legendary feats that he performed, things that are not possible. This should not be done. Recognize him for who he was, and do not try to deify him. When I met him, he was eighty-four years old, and he was still an utterly amazing martial artist. For me, that was enough to inspire my training and influence the rest of my life.

I owe all my teachers a great deal, as I would not be where I am today without them. They are dead now, but they still hold a place in my heart and my memories. I am forever grateful for the lessons that they taught me. In this text, I offer the insights that I have gained. I hope that they will benefit others who are following the path. We are all on the same mountain, striving to reach the summit.

Gambatte!

GLOSSARY OF TERMS

Aikido: A modern Japanese martial art founded by Ueshiba Morihei (1883-1969)

Aiuchi: Mutual death. It is a term used particularly in sword arts.

Ao: In modern Japanese, this is the word for blue, but originally, it referred to both blue and green.

Ate: Striking

Bijutsu: Art

Budo: The Japanese martial arts. The Sino-Japanese character literally means "martial way."

Bun bu ryo do: An expression meaning "the way of the brush is the same as the way of the sword.

Cha no yu: The tea ceremony

Chazen ichimi: Tea and Zen have the same flavor.

Chu: Loyalty

Daimyo: Feudal lords

Daito-ryu Aikijujutsu: A Japanese martial art, which was disseminated by Takeda Sokaku (1859-1943).

Dojo: Generally translated as training hall or training room, the literally definition is "place of the Way."

Dojo yaburi: tearing apart a martial arts training hall. Yaburi means "tearing" or "breaking."

Fudo-myoo: A Buddhist guardian king. His name literally means "immovable one." This deity originated in India, where it was known as Acalanatha or Acala Vidyaraja.

Fudoshin: Immovable mind

Funakogi undo: A "boat-rowing exercise" that originated in Chinese martial arts, but was adopted into Aikido.

Furitama: "Shaking the ball" exercise used in Aikido. Although adopted by the founder, Ueshiba Morihei, this practice originated in China. It is used to help loosen the tissue in the hara, freeing it up so that more movement, (and hence more power), is possible.

Gambaru: A Japanese verb meaning "work hard" and "persevere."

Genkan: Entryway.

Gi: Honor

Gotoku: The five virtues of Confucianism: *chu* (loyalty), *ko* (justice), *jin* (benevolence), *gi* (honor), and *rei* (respect, etiquette or courtesy)

Gyosho: A semi-cursive form of Japanese calligraphy

Hakama: Skirt-like trousers traditionally worn by Japanese men

Hakuda: Another name for jujutsu.

Hanmi: Half-body stance

Haori: Overcoat

Hara: The center, located in the abdomen. In the bodies of well-trained, internal martial artists, it is a mass of unified tissue that initiates all movement. In Chinese, this is known as the *dan t'ien.*

Hibiki: Resonance

Hombu: Head office, headquarters

Ichi go ichi e: One time, one meeting

Ikkyo: Technique number one.

Iku-musubi: Tying up the life force

Irori: The hearth found in the central room of traditional Japanese homes.

Isshin: One heart or one mind

Izakaya: Bars or drinking places in Japan

Jin: Benevolence

Jodan: A sword posture in which the blade is held above the head.

Kaisho: A print form of Japanese calligraphy

Kamiza: Literally, "top seat." It refers to small Shinto shrines found in homes and martial arts training halls.

Katamewaza: Pinning techniques

Kensho: Finding one's true nature.

Ki: Typically translated as "energy," this Sino-Japanese character also contains the following meanings: mind, disposition, nature, intention, and feeling, as evidenced by its use in many Japanese expressions.

Kiai: The guttural shout heard in traditional martial arts when practitioners attack or defend.

Kimono: Originally, this term just meant clothing in the Japanese language. Even in modern Japanese, the Sino-Japanese characters mean "thing that is worn." Typically, it refers to Japanese-style robes.

Kihaku: A type of eye-power or eye-energy that is said to be able to halt an attacker.

Kihon-waza: Basic techniques

Kime: Focus (of energy). Also, the peak (of energy).

Kintsukuroi: The art of piecing together broken pottery with gold or silver lacquer, thus making it even more beautiful.

Kito-ryu: A Japanese jujutsu style founded during the Edo Period (1868-1912).

Ko: Justice

Koan: Paradoxical statements or riddles that cannot be solved with the rational mind.

Kodo: Old martial ways

Kogusoku: Another name for jujutsu.

Kojiki: Record of ancient matters.

Kokyu: Breath

Koryu: Old schools. The term typically just refers to old-style Japanese martial arts.

Koshinage: Hip-throw

Kote hineri: This was the old term for an aikido technique known as sankyo. Kote was the armor that samurai used to protect the forearms and wrists. The term came to mean the forearm and wrist. Hineri means "twist" or "turn."

Kote mawashi: This refers to an aikido technique that is today known as nikkyo. Originally, kote was the term used to describe samurai armor that protected the forearms. By extension, this came to mean "forearm" and "wrist" in some Japanese martial arts. Mawashi means "turning" or "rotating."

Kotodama: Word spirits or word souls. This concept corresponds to the Christian notion of *logos*. (In the beginning, there was the Word, the Word was with God, and all things came into being through the Word.)

Kyudo: The art of archery

Maai: Interval, distance, and timing

Maitreya: The future Buddha

Metsuke: The term literally means "attaching the eyes," but refers to how to use the eyes and where to fix the eyes in combat.

Michi: The Way. An alternative pronunciation of the same Sino-Japanese character is Do.

Miko: Japanese shaman

Misogi: Purification

Mudansha: Unranked students. In most martial traditions, this refers to students who have not earned a black belt.

Mushin: No-mind

Musubi: Tying

Nagewaza: Throwing techniques

Namu: "I take refuge in…"

Nihon Shoki: Chronicles of Japan

Nijiriguchi: Crawling-in entrance

Nikkyo: Technique number two

Ofudesaki: Literally "from the tip of the brush." This is also the lengthy holy text of Omoto-kyo, written by a Deguchi Nao (1836 – 1918).

Osoto-gari: Outer leg-reap. It is a Judo technique

Randori: Free practice

Rei: Respect, bow, courtesy, gratitude, or appreciation

Sabi: Unpolished beauty

Sado: A literal definition of this term is "the way of tea." Sometimes, the word is used to refer to the tea ceremony (*cha no yu*) itself.

Samadhi: High level of meditative concentration

Samu: Physical work done with complete focus.

Samurai: A class of Japanese warriors. The Sino-Japanese character depicts a person together with a temple, so *samurai* has the inherent meaning of "one who serves."

Sangha: The community of Buddhist monks and nuns

Sankaku-tai: Triangular body or stance

Sankin kotai: An ordinance put into place by the Tokugawa Shogunate, which required feudal lords to spend every third year in the capital. When they were not there, their heirs had to remain. In effect, it was a hostage system.

Sankyo: Technique number three

Sarei: Rules of etiquette for the Tea Ceremony

Sempai: A respectful title used for one's seniors (upperclassmen).

Sen: Initiative

Sengoku jidai: The Warring States Period

Shakuhachi: A Japanese bamboo flute

Shibui: Astringent

Shibui-kawa: Astringent skin

Shibui konomi: An inherent appreciation of the elements, properly arranged and balanced, which are found centered in art, and in one's life and personality.

Shibumi: Astringency

Shihan: High-ranking martial art instructors. The term conveys the sense of "role-model."

Shiho-hai: A symbolic act of demonstrating gratitude to the four cardinal directions which is performed in some Shinto ceremonies.

Shiho-nage: Four-direction throw, which is found in Aikido

Shimewaza: Choking techniques

Shin: Sincerity, heart, or mind, depending upon the Sino-Japanese character used to represent it.

Shinsengumi: A group of warriors that existed until the Meiji Restoration and Commodore Perry's visit.

Shinto: The animistic native faith of Japan

Shizentai: Natural posture

Shodan: In most martial traditions, a first-degree black belt. The Sino-Japanese characters literally mean "beginning rank."

Shodo: Literally, "the way of writing," it can also be translated as "calligraphy."

Shubaku: Another name for jujutsu

Shugyo: Training. The word is often used specifically with the goal of spiritual progress in mind.

Soke: Inheritor

Sosho: A cursive form of Japanese calligraphy

Suibokuga: Water charcoal painting

Suigetsu: Moon and water. It is often translated as "the moon abiding on water," and it is an important high-level concept in the martial arts.

Sumi-e: Japanese ink painting

Tai no henka: Body change

Tai sabaki: Body movement

Taijutsu: Another name for jujutsu

Tainai kuguri: An ascetic practice involving entering caves used by Shugendo adherents. The term literally means, "to pass through the womb."

Takenouchi-ryu: The oldest jujutsu system in Japan, founded during the Muromachi Period (1336-1573).

Tanden: An energy point in the lower abdomen.

Tatami: Straw mats used as flooring in Japanese style rooms.

Tegoi: An ancient Japanese martial art. Little is known of its techniques or practices.

Tenchijin: Heaven, earth, and humankind

Tenchinage: Heaven and earth throw, which is found in Aikido.

Tokonoma: Alcove in which flowers and a hanging scroll are traditionally placed.

Torii: Large gates, which mark the entrance of a Shinto shrine.

Torite: Another name for jujutsu.

Tsukuri: Fitting in. It refers to how a judo practitioner moves his body after breaking his opponent's balance, so that he can execute a throw.

Ude osae: Literally, "arm control," Ueshiba originally used this term to describe an elbow-controlling technique in aikido, which is today known as *ikkyo*.

Wa: Harmony

Wabi: Refined elegance

Waza: A general term meaning "techniques."

Yakuza: An impolite term used to describe Japanese gangsters

Yama arashi: Mountain storm. It was the name of an old Judo technique that is not usually practiced in modern dojo.

Yawara: Another name for jujutsu

Yudansha: Ranked students. In most martial arts, black belt rank or higher.

Zanshin: Remaining mind

Zensho: Zen Calligraphy

NOTES

1   Kano, *Kodokan Judo*, 23.

2   Ibid., 25.

3   DeProspero & DeProspero, *Illuminated Spirit*, 124.

4   Kano, *Mind over Muscle*, 34.

5   http://judoinfo.com/new/alphabetical-list/categorywisey-index/103-people-in-judo/598-memories-of-my-sensei-takahiko-ishikawa-9th-dan.

6   Yamamoto, *Hagakure*, 81.

7   Skoss, *Koryu Bujutsu*, 50.

8   Funakoshi, *Karate-Do*.

9   Ueshiba, *A Life in Aikido*, 19-20.

10 Takuan, *Unfettered Mind*, 22.

11 Ibid., 30 – 31.

12 Reps, *Zen Flesh, Zen Bones*, 244.

13 Ibid., 256.

14 Stevens, *Sacred Calligraphy of the East*, 143.

15 Okumura, *Aikido Today Magazine*, no. 41.

16 http://www.aikidofaq.com/misc/hakama.html.

17 http://www.shibuiswords.com/ancientStudyNihonto.htm.

18 Pranin, *Aikido Pioneers*, 275.

19 Ibid., 276.

20 Ibid., 278.

21 Pranin, *Koichi Tohei*, Aikido Journal #110 (www.aikidojournal.com/article?article=35)

22 Pranin, *Aikido Pioneers*, 278.

23 http://www.aikidosangenkai.org/blog/morihei-ueshiba-untranslatable-words/#.UgRKsMvD_tw.

24 Ibid.

25 "Interview with Shogen Okabayashi," www.aikidojournal.com.

26 Sagawa, *Transparent Power*, 150.

27 Ibid., 149.

28 http://www.oomoto.jp/enDokon/main.html.

29 Quoted in Ueshiba, *A Life in Aikido*, 218.

30 Sagawa, *Transparent Power*, 149.

31 Yagyu, *Life Giving Sword*, 107.

32 Tohei, *Ki in Daily Life*, 20.

33 From *Aikido Journal*, volume 25, no. 3, 13.

34 Pranin, *Aikido Pioneers*, 122.

35 Wilson, *Lone Samurai*, 178-179.

36 Stevens, *Abundant Peace*.

37 Ibid.

38 Ibid.

39 Ibid., 154.

40 Ibid., 154.

41 Yamamoto, *Hagakure*, 99.

42 Ueshiba, *A Life in Aikido*, 307-308.

43 Ibid., 311.

44 Reps & Sasaki, *Zen Flesh, Zen Bones*, 177 – 178.

45 Ibid., 186-187.

46 Stevens, *Abundant Peace*, 94.

47 Ueshiba, *Takemusu Aiki*, 21.

48 Pranin, *Aikido Pioneers*, 126.

49 Gleason, *Spiritual Foundations*, 59.

50 Ueshiba, *Takemusu Aiki*, 19.

51 Ueshiba, *A Life in Aikido*, 315.

52 Ibid.

53 Suzuki, *Zen and Japanese Culture*.

54 Lao Tzu, *Tao Te Ching*, 63.

55 Okakura, *The Book of Tea*, 55.

56 Ibid., 45.

57 Yasuhiko, "Development of the Chanoyu," 28.

58 Kumakura, "Sen no Rikyu," 51.

59 Jeremiah, *Living Buddhas*.

60 Mann, *When Buddhists Attack*.

61 Ibid.

62 Okakura, *Book of Tea*, 122–123.

63 Yamamoto, *Hagakure*, 46.

BIBLIOGRAPHY

Gleason, W. *The Spiritual Foundations of Aikido*. Vermont: Destiny Books, 1995.

Jeremiah, K. *Living Buddhas: The Self-Mummified Monks of Yamagata, Japan*. North Carolina: McFarland & Co., Inc., 2010.

Kano, J. *Kodokan Judo*. Tokyo: Kodansha, 1986.

Kano, J. *Mind over Muscle: Writings from the Founder of Judo*. Tokyo: Kodansha, 2005.

Kimura, T. *Transparent Power: A Secret Teaching Revealed*. San Fransiscio, CA: MAAT Press, 2009.

Kumakura, I. "Sen no Rikyu: Inquiries into his life and tea." (Translated by P. Varley). In *Tea in Japan: Essays on the History of Chanoyu*, (pp. 33-67). Edited by P. Varley and Isao Kumakura, 1995.

Lao Tzu. *Tao Te Ching*. (translated by R. B. Blakney). New York: Mentor Books, 1955.

Mann, J. *When Buddhists Attack: The Curious Relationship between Zen and the Martial Arts*. Vermont: Tuttle & Co., Inc., 2012.

Okakura, K. *The Book of Tea*. Boston: Shambala, 1993.

Pranin, S. *Aikido Pioneers, Pre-War Era*. Tokyo: Aiki News, 2010.

Pranin, S. Morihei Ueshiba and Sokaku Takeda. *Aiki News, 94*, 1993.

Reps, P. & Senzaki, N. *Zen Flesh, Zen Bones*. Boston, Shambala, 1994.

Saotome, M. *Aikido and the Harmony of Nature*. Boston: Shambala, 1993.

Sharp, H. "Memories of My Sensei, Takahiko Ishikawa, 9th dan." *Judo Info*. Retrieved from http://judoinfo.com/ishikawa.htm.

Skoss, M. "The meaning of martial arts training: A conversation with Sawada Hanae." In Skoss, D., Ed., *Koryu Bujutsu: Classical Warrior Traditions of Japan*. New Jersey: Koryu Books, 1995.

Stevens, J. *The Sword of No-Sword: Life of the Master Warrior Tesshu*. Boston: Shambhala, 1984.

Stevens, J. *Abundant Peace: The Biography of Morihei Ueshiba, Founder of Aikido*. Boston, Shambhala, 1987.

Stevens, J. (Ed.). *The Essence of Aikido: Spiritual Teachings of Morihei Ueshiba*. Tokyo: Kodansha, 1993.

Stevens, J. *The Secrets of Aikido*. Boston: Shambhala, 1995.

Stevens, J. *Sacred Calligraphy of the East*. Boston: Shambhala, 1995.

Stevens, J. *The Way of Judo: A Portrait of Jigoro Kano and his Students*. Boston: Shambhala, 2013.

Suzuki, D. T. *Zen and Japanese Culture*. New Jersey: Princeton University Press, 2010.

Takuan, S. *The Unfettered Mind: Writings of the Zen Master to the Sword Master*. W. Wilson, Trans.). Tokyo: Kodansha, 1986.

Tohei, K. *Ki in Daily Life*. Tokyo: Ki no Kenkyukai, 1978.

Ueshiba, K. *A Life in Aikido: The Biography of Founder Morihei Ueshiba*. (K. Izawa & M. Fuller, Trans.). Tokyo: Kodansha, 2008.

Ueshiba, M. *The Art of Peace*. (J. Stevens, Trans.). Tokyo, Kodansha, 1992.

Ueshiba, M. *Budo: Teachings of the Founder of Aikido*. (J. Stevens, Trans.). Tokyo: Kodansha, 1996.

Ueshiba, M. "Takemusu Aiki." *Aikido Journal, 26*(2), 18-21, 1999.

Wilson, W. *The Lone Samurai: The Life of Miyamoto Musashi*. Tokyo: Kodansha, 2004.

Yagyu, M. *The Life-Giving Sword: Secret Teachings from the House of the Shogun*. (W. Wilson, Trans.). Tokyo: Kodansha, 2003.

Yasuhiko, M. "The development of the Chanoyu." (Translated by P. Varley). In *Tea in Japan: Essays on the History of Chanoyu*, (pp. 3-32). Edited by P. Varley and Isao Kumakura, 1995.

Made in the USA
Middletown, DE
25 October 2023

41388194R00156